THE
CHALUPA
RULES

D0957903

THE
CHALUPA
RULES

A Latino Guide to
GRINGOLANDIA

MARIO BÓSQUEZ

A PLUME BOOK

PLUME
Published by Penguin Group
Penguin Group (USA) Inc., 375 Hudson Street, New York,
New York 10014, U.S.A.
Penguin Group (Canada), 10 Alcorn Avenue, Toronto, Ontario, Canada
M4V 3B2 (a division of Pearson Penguin Canada Inc.)
Penguin Books Ltd., 80 Strand, London WC2R 0RL, England
Penguin Ireland, 25 St. Stephen's Green,
Dublin 2, Ireland (a division of Penguin Books Ltd.)
Penguin Group (Australia), 250 Camberwell Road, Camberwell, Victoria 3124,
Australia (a division of Pearson Australia Group Pty. Ltd.)
Penguin Books India Pvt. Ltd., 11 Community Centre,
Panchsheel Park, New Delhi – 110 017, India
Penguin Books (NZ), cnr Airborne and Rosedale Roads, Albany,
Auckland 1310, New Zealand (a division of Pearson New Zealand Ltd.)
Penguin Books (South Africa) (Pty.) Ltd., 24 Sturdee Avenue, Rosebank,
Johannesburg 2196, South Africa

Penguin Book Ltd., Registered Offices: 80 Strand, London WC2R 0RL,
England

First published by Plume, a member of Penguin Group (USA) Inc.

First Printing, May 2005
10 9 8 7 6 5 4 3 2 1

Copyright © Mario Bósquez, 2005
All rights reserved

Ⓟ REGISTERED TRADEMARK—MARCA REGISTRADA

CIP data ia available.
ISBN 0-452-28608-5

Printed in the United States of America
Set in New Baskerville
Designed by Eve L. Kirch

Without limiting the rights under copyright reserved above, no part of this publication may be reproduced, stored in or introduced into a retrieval system, or transmitted, in any form, or by any means (electronic, mechanical, photocopying, recording, or otherwise), without the prior written permission of both the copyright owner and the above publisher of this book.

PUBLISHER'S NOTE
The scanning, uploading, and distribution of this book via the Internet or via any other means without the permission of the publisher is illegal and punishable by law. Please purchase only authorized electronic editions, and do not participate in or encourage electronic piracy of copyrighted materials. Your support of the author's rights is appreciated.

BOOKS ARE AVAILABLE AT QUANTITY DISCOUNTS WHEN USED TO PROMOTE PRODUCTS OR SERVICES. FOR INFORMATION PLEASE WRITE TO PREMIUM MARKETING DIVISION, PENGUIN GROUP (USA) INC., 375 HUDSON STREET, NEW YORK, NEW YORK 10014

For Nana, *Inez Alcalá Bósquez, mother, friend, and guide-to-life.*
Thank you for showing us how to live. This book is for you.

ACKNOWLEDGMENTS

The Chalupa Rules is dedicated to all of our ancestors, Latino and otherwise, who gave us wisdom and advice in the form of sayings and proverbs.

Special thanks to all *mi familia* or, as I lovingly call them, "My Favorite Mexicans." *Mis hermanas, muchas gracias:* Irene, Imelda, Elena, Susanna, and María Elia (we made it out together!). My love for you is beyond words. A big *abrazo* to all my brothers-in-law.

My niece, best friend, and coconspirator, Alexandra Alcalá aka Sister, thanks for the love, support, and help with the illustrations. Among the first words she ever spoke: "You sing, I dance, okay?!" It's been that way ever since. Much love to all my nieces and nephews: Matthew, Mitchell, Max, Aaron, Ashlee, and Erica. You are my *corazónes también.*

For my *tía* Elia who taught me that there is "no science," that everything is possible. I think of you every day.

A huge *gracias*, a big *abrazo* to my agent, friend, and Latina powerhouse, Johanna Castillo of Sanford J. Greenburger Associates. Thank you for seeing the power and potential in *The Chalupa Rules*. I couldn't have done it without you.

A great, big *abrazo y gracias* to Jake Klisivitch, associate editor at Plume. I am forever grateful for your talent, insight, and contributions to this book. Even though you are Canadian you are also now and forever one of "My Favorite Mexicans."

For my *abuelita*, Toribia Cortinas-Bósquez, *gracias* for the *dichos*, herbs, and healing. For my father, Tomás C. Bósquez.

To my wonderful friends Lisa Quiroz, Donna Parker-Bannwolf, Bruce Maniscalco, Charlie Pérez and family, Cindy Leal Massey , Mike Carmona, Lizz and Marilyn Salaway, Becky Chavarría-Chaives, Mary McGee, Allen and Lyn Horowitz, Lyn Brown, Sandy Jeffries, Carol Jenkins, Ray Parisi, Joe Fusco, David Thompsen, Dr. Janet Shefts, my broadcast agent Mark Turner, and so many more *amigos y amigas*.

A very special *abrazo* for Jack Hyman and David and Gail Gifford, *amigos* who are more Mexican than even I am, thanks for decorating my life.

To my WCBS *familia,* especially president and general manager Lew Leone, and senior vice president and news director Dianne Doctor.

Abrazos for Dave Price, Shon Gables, Vanessa Alfano, Audrey Puente, Lynda López, Duke Castiglione, Brett Larsen, Jeff Berardelli, and all the WCBS staff and crew, in particular Cindy Hsu for her warm inquiries, "How's the book coming?"

To Sung Chu Mei restaurant in Manhattan for keeping me supplied with Orange-Flavored Beef and Crystal Shrimp Dumplings through the long nights of writing and editing. For my dog Huitzi, friend, roommate, and co–Chinese food eater.

And to Diana Rodríguez, wherever you are.

CONTENTS

PREFACE

9:59:00 p.m. Eastern time.

A New York City television studio.

The scripts are written and the cameras are in position. The field correspondents are poised to deliver their live reports. The news anchor walks into the studio and takes his place behind the news desk. Bathed in bright lights, he places the microphone on his lapel and makes his final preparations to deliver the news.

How am I going to make it through another week? I'm down to loose change and baloney sandwiches once again.

The news anchor reviews his copy one last time. He takes a deep breath and waits for the stage manager's cue. Another news broadcast in the nation's number one television market is about to begin. Stories and video about natural disasters, politics, and world events are transmitted into New Yorkers' homes one more time. He moves from story to story; trusting that over two decades in the television industry will help him deliver the news with the highest level of confidence and professionalism.

Will they somehow be able to tell that I grew up in three rooms with no hot water? That eight people were crammed into that tiny space? That many times we lived on bags of donated clothes and groceries?

The studio lights forgive nothing. The camera lenses take

in everything. The wardrobe seems to be in order; the suit, tie, and hair appropriate for the image of a news anchor.

I hope they don't notice the faded parts of this old blazer. I'm glad they can't see the shirt underneath with its frayed collar, yellowing buttons and holes at each elbow.

It's time to make the transition to the weather forecast. Friendly banter between the newscaster and the meteorologist goes smoothly. There are smiles all around as the anchor transfers the show into the weatherman's hands. Adjusting his tie and straightening his back, the news anchor waits for his turn to speak.

My hands are shaking. If I clasp them together really tight maybe it won't show. Under the glaring lights of a New York City television studio, dark memories reach out and grab me, rattling my self-confidence. I am glad the cameras can't see the violent domestic fights, the drunken rages, and years of poverty that pock-marked my childhood.

The newscast proceeds smoothly. The anchorman seems secure, at ease. He knows he is working with the best directors, writers, photographers, and editors in the business. During the show, they all make plans to "hang out" after the broadcast.

How will I explain that I can't have dinner with them after the show? I'll claim to be tired, exhausted from a long day's work. That way I won't have to tell them I'm broke.

The newscast is over. It's time for a quick meeting to review the program. Walking briskly, the newsman heads toward his small one-bedroom apartment seven blocks away from the studio.

It's small and cramped but it's perfect. Close enough to work to avoid having to spend money on transportation and hey, it has hot, running water. For my family, that's a luxury. I can't forget how good it felt when we finally moved into a new home of our own. The FHA 235 government-sponsored home featured three bedrooms, front and back yards, and enough space for eight family members; a boost to our living quarters and our self-esteem.

And now here he is in the Big Apple, *La Gran Manzana*. Those years of high school plays, speech contests, and writing classes seem to have paid off for New York City's first full-time Chicano news anchor.

No, he's not network and not prime time. Nonetheless, he's proud of what he does and equally proud of what he doesn't do. He escaped the cycle of heavy drinking that plagued his family. He broke the chain of domestic violence that scarred his childhood. He worked his way out of hand-outs and hands-across-the-face.

Most important of all, he doesn't repeat those mistakes.

The man in the frayed, much-repaired business suit and worn-out shoes isn't anything special. He's just a working guy who's earning a living, like everyone else. However, his "road to normal" was far from easy.

And he didn't do it alone. The New York City television journalist had a lifetime of help from family and friends. He also learned sayings and proverbs that offer advice, counseling, and comfort. Actually they got him to New York, one *dicho* at a time.

Like other Latinos, this fourth-generation Chicano never lets go of the Spanish proverbs that light the way to success. As a matter of fact, this Mexican American takes it one step further. He has his own handcrafted, homemade proverbs. Those sayings, those *dichos*, are imprinted on his mind with the help of powerful, unforgettable images from a simple Mexican game of chance known to many as *Lotería*. But in South Texas, where he is from, the game is known as *La Chalupa*.

He may work in big-city television but his heart is rooted in his culture, his history, and his family. And, just because he has a job people might perceive as a sign of success, that doesn't mean he is not still struggling. The secret to his survival is the philosophy on life he calls "The Chalupa Rules."

So, while he goes about his work, trying to make it in the

big city, no one has to know he feels like the newest chicken in the henhouse, has a beggar's body, and swims in two cultures.

I am that New York City television journalist. Without this "Guide to Gringolandia," I never would have survived the violence, the hunger, and the discrimination. It's time to share my story so that someone else's journey can be easier. These are my Chalupa Rules. Grab them. Take them in. Put them into practice. They come from years of trial and error, days of despair, and months of worry. They work if you listen closely to what they say.

Yes, life can be very tough for Latinos and other minorities here in the United States. Yes, you'll hear words of bigotry and taste the bitterness of loss, but you can work your way through all of this.

The Chalupa Rules come from my *corazón.* When we share our experiences, we realize "Hey, I'm not alone in this. I am not the only one who struggles. This guy may work in New York and have a nice job, but he is also no stranger to discrimination and to pinching pennies until they scream."

Before we go any further, let me explain the traditional game that inspires the Chalupa Rules.

To many Mexicans and other Latinos, this game of chance is sometimes called *Lotería.* But to South Texas Chicanos, the game is named after one of its playing cards. The image is of a beautiful Mexican woman, rowing a little boat known by the name *Chalupa.* Yes, it is also the name of a famous Tex-Mex dish. Chalupas are crispy-fried corn tortillas topped with refried beans and melted cheese.

The other playing cards feature the sun, plants, animals, and fantastic creatures from the world of Mexican folklore. The matching deck of cards features the same images. The one who calls out the cards must recite a saying or riddle that hints at its identity. Players use pinto beans as markers and cover the matching image on their game card. The first to fill it up, wins. The images and some proverbs from this traditional game inspired *The Chalupa Rules.*

In the pages that follow, the Chalupa Rules are laid out like this. There is an *Imagen*, or image, inspired by the cards used to play the game of Mexican bingo. It will help you remember the rule.

There is a *Dicho*. The Chalupa Rule featured in the chapter is printed in Spanish and in English.

Then there is the *Prontito*. To Tex-Mexicans it means "in a little hurry." If you don't have time just read the bold-face paragraphs, grab on to the spirit of the Chalupa Rule *prontito*, and then be on your way.

When you do have time, there is *A Lo Largo*, the at-length description of the Chalupa Rule so you can really dive into its heart and get all the *jugo*, all of the juice that it has to offer.

Oye, mira. Look here. Don't expect teams of experts and mountains of research, reports, and statistics. I didn't learn these Chalupa Rules from a piece of paper. I *lived* these Rules, by watching my mother get hit, by seeing my sisters go hungry, and by getting slammed by discrimination. I lived them by figuring out how to get an education, launch and maintain a career, and support my family. I did it by linking the Mexican game of bingo, traditional Spanish proverbs, and my own "handcrafted" rules.

We've never met, but you know me. I'm the Latino kid in your *barrio*, the one wearing the faded hand-me-downs and living in a crowded house. The child who tries to smile in spite of the screaming and fighting at home.

I'm the *pobrecito*, the "poor little one" who is the recipient of everyone's pity, the one with potential but no future. I'm your son, your nephew, your neighbor's little kid. This description also fits your daughter, your niece, or any little girl who has to navigate tremendous obstacles in order to make her voice heard. You know me. You might even be just like me. *Ay, ay, ay.* Don't lecture me, you might say. That's not what this is about. It's about sharing and getting a handle on how to deal with situations larger than yourself, alien to how you grew up.

Emceeing a gala at the legendary Waldorf-Astoria hotel in

Manhattan and meeting Gloria Estefan on the same night can make anyone shake in their *botas*.

Fine, no problem. Call up the Chalupa Rule that says, *No seas como pollo recién comprado.* "Don't be like the newest chicken in the henhouse." Don't make yourself small. You have a *right* to be here.

There are thirty chapters of Chalupa Rules included in this guide to *Gringolandia*. They are easy to remember if you memorize the image that goes along with each one. It's like a menu at a Mexican restaurant with pictures for every entrée. Memorize the picture and they come to mind much easier. If you like the food analogy (and who doesn't like Mexican food?) picture a little taco stand and me behind the counter, tossing the ingredients of my Chalupa Rules onto the griddle. I cook them up and serve them to you, "homemade"; fresh from my mind to yours.

Eat them while they're hot. Fatten up your self-confidence until it becomes *gordito*, chubby with insights and advice that might help you achieve your goals.

Are you ready? Will you let a sultry mermaid, a vigilant soldier, or a wide-eyed frog give you advice in life? You will, if you let this book guide your way. *The Chalupa Rules: A Latino's Guide to Gringolandia* maps out a way for Latinos to navigate life in the United States while always holding on to the history and values of our ancestors.

Even though I am the first ever full-time Chicano news anchor in New York City, I really should have been the "least likely to succeed." Everything stood in my way. Poverty, domestic violence, and discrimination threatened to shatter my struggling family into a million pieces. My professional life in television journalism wasn't any easier. Television news in 1978, when I first started, wasn't exactly an open playground of opportunity for young Chicanos.

I have heard it all:
You don't look Mexican enough.

You look too Mexican.

You sound too Mexican.

You can go home now.

I may go home for vacation, family emergencies, or holidays, but never in the defeat that might have come from succumbing to racism or bigotry.

I was born in Alice, Texas, where, during my early years, we lived in a small house with no hot water, very little space, and an outhouse. We didn't have much money but had a strong work ethic, deep family bonds, and our sayings or *dichos* that older relatives taught us. We were poor, but had strong family values. Our amusements were few and inexpensive, a simple game of baseball, tag, or perhaps hide-and-seek. In addition, our game of Chalupa lifted our spirits and inspired us.

I struggled my way through my elementary, junior high, and high school years as I dealt with the shattering family situations that challenged my sisters and me every single day. We went to school knowing that domestic violence, abuse of alcohol, and poverty awaited us when school was over and we had to return home. I was saved from following an almost unbroken chain of violent drinkers by incredibly strong family members and by my Chalupa Rules that offer insights and solutions to many of life's problems and challenges. You, too, can overcome these problems if you are willing to invest the time to take in rules that were born out of necessity.

I worked in radio as a newscaster and news director and at the same time threw a paper route for grocery money. I co-hosted a magazine show, taking exotic trips while living in a government-sponsored "FHA 235" home. I was a television reporter and anchor who also worked at theme parks for much-needed, extra funds.

I anchored the news in New York City while turning a blind eye to all the fancy restaurants and clothing stores that tempt you every step of the way. I was simply too broke to even go through their doors. Almost every penny of my surplus money went home to Texas.

Every time I face what appear to be insurmountable obstacles, I recall a Mexican saying that fits the situation.

If I am distracted at work and tempted to let my mind wander, *A lo que te truje Chencha* surfaces to make me concentrate and get the job done faster. This phrase is a Tex-Mex way of saying, "Do what you came here to do, focus." It reminds me to think of nothing else but the task at hand.

I want to share my Chalupa Rules to prove you can have a career and conquer ghosts and demons of a disadvantaged past. There is a sense of relief when you find out, "Wow. I am not the only one going through that." I provide insight for fellow Latinos with the stories that accompany my Chalupa Rules. These insights helped this kid from the South Texas *barrios* to become a news anchor in New York City. In reality, the path that led to my career was paved well before I was born.

The Latinos who came before us—those who worked and sweated in the fields, those who endured racism and abuse, and those who offered up wise sayings for us to follow—are the ones who laid the foundation for our futures. We must not let them down. These are their Chalupa Rules.

Some of the *dichos* ring out from the back of the traditional playing cards. Others are voices from the past; your own ancestors whispering valuable advice into your ear. The rest I created, drawing from a lifetime of trying to survive.

It's extremely reassuring that I can type some of the traditional Chalupa Rules into an Internet search engine and they pop up on the screen. Their meaning may vary from region to region but still they are there, stored away for safekeeping in cyberspace.

It's nice to know that they are easily within reach, bubbling away with their insight and meaning, as comforting as a simmering pot of *frijoles* cooking away on *Abuelita*'s stove.

Well, the ingredients are all mixed together and they are sizzling.

Let me grab a tortilla and make you a little taco, stuffed with the spice of cultural heritage, the meat of our identity, and the flavoring that comes from all the places where Latinos hold their heads high. Let me share my Chalupa Rules with you. Taste them. Savor them.

¡Provecho!

INTRODUCTION

The Birth of the Chalupa Rules

There isn't much color in some parts of South Texas, where I was born. There's the dust, khaki-colored and stinging when wind storms whip it up. There are also the pale green, razor-thin leaves of the mesquite trees. They produce anemic-yellow bean pods that, in the summer, bake into hollow, brown rattles; nature's maracas when the South Texas wind rakes through the branches. You have to scratch the surface to find the true colors of the Texas where I grew up.

Slice open a ripe, extravagantly fat watermelon and you're rewarded by a deep, sweet red that dares you to look away from its ruby brilliance. Wait until Easter Sunday and all the modest, wood-frame homes hatch little *niñas* wearing their holiday best. They are excited, dancing rainbows of colors that push the envelope of what's usually considered "pastel." Their frilly, fussy dresses blush with the innocence of canary-yellow, mint green, and robin's-egg blue.

The colors of my South Texas also lay dormant in a simple cardboard box that is usually shoved under a bed or parked on a dark, musty closet shelf next to strings of sleeping Christmas lights and fiesta decorations that wait patiently for their turn to once again illuminate, amuse, and delight. Pick up the box and shake it. You'll hear a hundred or more little tapping sounds as the contents wake up at the prospect of a rousing game of Mexican bingo. The chubby pinto beans dance around the inside of the box, anxious to act out their role as markers in the game.

Shake the box again and you will hear the deck of cards as they slide around, hitting the sides of the container. They rap and knock impatiently, trying to coax you in letting them come out to play. The entire cast of characters is already in full Mexican costume, ready to appear on the stage of this game of chance.

Lift the lid and meet them.

There's *El Catrín*. The starchy, overdressed dandy poses delicately in his impeccable white tie and tails. Here's *La Sirena*, the most innocently voluptuous mermaid you will ever meet. Her shiny, raven hair makes not even the slightest attempt to cover the perfect, bare breasts she offers to the world. *La Sirena* seems to be enjoying the frothy bubble bath of water that her glossy tail has whipped up around her.

There's *El Valiente*, the brave one. This overtly macho man seems to have paused in the middle of a bar brawl to glare at you while you play the game. His eyes promise a fight to the finish. His muscular chest heaves from the exertion of being so *valiente*. The deck of playing cards also includes *La Chalupa* herself. She is resplendent in her traditional Mexican dress; her colorful, off-the-shoulder peasant Aztec blouse frames a beautiful face. She rows a small boat, her *chalupa* as it is called in Spanish, with a look of pride on her face. Aboard the boat are lush fruits and flowers that are the ripe bounty of a successful harvest.

These characters from the Mexican world of imagery are joined by many others. Some are simple and some are audacious. They all demand your undivided attention.

You will meet the big, fat *Rana*/the Frog; the prim, svelte *Dama*/the Lady; and the empty, haunting eye sockets and forbidding countenance of *La Muerte*/Death.

The cast of players in Mexican bingo make the U.S. version of the game seem, by comparison, suffocating and boring. How can flat, black-and-white letters and numbers ever compete with the Mexican playing cards that shout and sing of everything from a bright, red devil to a proud rooster crowing his handsomeness to the world?

It was this potent game of chance, full of proverbs and promise, that we played as children. All we knew at the time was that someone had to be the "caller," in charge of shuffling the deck of cards and then calling them out, one by one.

"¡El Árbol!" "¡La Estrella!" "¡El Mundo!" We listened with the concentrated power of fervent believers as we waited, a pinto bean marker poised in our sweaty little hands. We waited to see if the card being called out was a match for a space on our playing card. When someone eventually filled in their entire card with pinto beans (or pennies if there was extra money in the family to throw around), they would greedily shout, "Chalupa!" and claim the coveted prize of a pile of pinto beans or stack of pennies, whichever served as the treasure for the night.

It would go something like this:

It's a hot summer night in South Texas. Alice, Texas, to be exact. A gaggle of young cousins has convened in front of the small, wood house that's bursting at the seams with Mexicans. The *primos* range in age from five to fifteen and we all have the thirsty look of rabid Chalupa players in our eyes. We all carefully squat or sit on the red concrete porch that, even at night, is still baking from a day's worth of summer sun but it's better than sitting on the grass. Even though the blades are cool to the touch and provide a soft, springy cushion for our bony bottoms, there are also *chinches*, tiny mites that bite and burrow into our skin and threaten an entire night of itchy discomfort. So instead, we sacrifice our young skins to the heat of the concrete porch.

Our cousin Cecilia is the designated "caller" for our game of Chalupa. Her voice gets lost in the raspy mating calls of the thousands of *chicharras*/cicadas that hide in the darkness of the South Texas night and provide a noisy cheering section as our game rages on. She pulls a card from the deck and calls out its identity. *"La Sirena!"* she shouts as we hoot and laugh at the outrageous nudity Cecilia holds up before us. Our assortment of blue, green, hazel, and brown eyes train themselves on the raucous colors that make up the mermaid's extravagant display of lush black hair and ripe, red fish tail that slaps at the water that surrounds her. We marvel at how she is a creature of two elements: air and water. Perhaps we react to this card in such a strong manner because we too are creatures of two worlds: Mexico and the United States.

We all search for *La Sirena* on our playing cards.

Perhaps the mermaid would lead our way to victory. You would think we were playing for the crown jewels of England. There is a mound of freckled pinto beans at dead center of the game. That's the treasure we are lusting after; the *frijoles* that are the Holy Grail of our noisy, often contentious game of chance. That is how we played Chalupa, the visual foundation for my rules of life.

I grew up poor, surrounded by domestic violence and heavy drinking. I was the kid everyone felt sorry for, the one who mowed lawns and cleaned rich people's houses to support his family. I've spent a lifetime wearing hand-me-downs too big or too small for me, but the only clothes I had. I spent years pretending I wasn't hungry so that my family could eat.

Success is not always measured by headline-grabbing achievement or box-office receipts. Success, in our family, was surviving another day without getting kicked out of our house or yet another day without watching one of us getting kicked around.

There is no neat, crisp line of division between my turbulent, formative years and my work as a broadcast journalist. There is no well-defined "border" that I had to cross from struggling financially and recovering from childhood trauma into my present job as a New York City television anchor. I struggle to survive, to this very day.

Census Bureau numbers in the year 2000 reported over thirty-five million Latinos in the United States. In that number are countless dreams, aspirations, and hopes for the future. We look to others for inspiration and sometimes we read about a person's life experiences and they seem glossy yet attainable. But the waters are rarely smooth and friendly. Oftentimes we encounter storms at sea and whirlpools of procrastination, temptation, and weakness that threaten to sink our dreams.

In the Chalupa Rules that follow, I take cues from my own culture and upbringing to cope with life in the United States. I put all my "cards" on the table, open for inspection so that you can learn from my experience.

I look at the "Lady of the Chalupa," the beautiful woman rowing the small boat that gives her name to this Mexican game of chance, and I see someone who is rowing her way through life with all the riches of the Mexican harvest aboard. Like her, I load up my own rowboat with a valuable bounty. Like I've described for you, the harvest that I share with you comes from the back of Chalupa playing cards, old Mexican proverbs and my own rules of life. They are "The Chalupa Rules." Through them, you will get insight as to how a Mexican kid from the *barrio* ended up as a communicator in the number one television market in the world.

Am I bragging a little? You better believe it. To find out why, read the first chapter, *El Gallo*/The Rooster and learn how, as Latinos, we need to crow more about our achievements.

Even as I write this, my New York City apartment is drenched in oranges and yellows, Mexican artwork and Native American masks. I even joke about how it looks like a "mariachi threw up in it." I drape myself in my culture and proclaim it to the world. But I was not always that way. The

Chalupa Rules helped me embrace my own culture, while at the same time making it through what could be called *Gringolandia*. Find out how *La Sirena*, the Mermaid, can help you swim in your own cultural waters.

Be prepared for the bright, shocking colors of Mexican imagery and candid details from my life of struggle. The colors of my South Texas include the rainbow of reds, blues, and greens of Mexican bingo. I couldn't have survived without *El Sol, La Luna,* and *El Valiente* and the rewarding *dichos*/sayings that inspired me to unite them all under the banner of the Chalupa Rules.

One of the rules instructs: *Deten la Bandera*/Hold on to your flag. Through storms, through abuse, through struggle hold on to your own banner that represents your most precious goals and dreams. Never let it drop. It may get dark sometimes. Clouds may dim your view of the goals that you have set. But if you read the following pages, the Sun and the Moon of the Chalupa will light your way.

CHALUPA RULE ONE

1

EL GALLO
The Rooster

Don't Act Like the Newest Chicken in the Henhouse

No Seas Como Pollo Recién Comprado

Prontito:

Are you terrified to speak in front of your coworkers or fellow students? Does the thought of meeting new people make you cringe? Then this Chalupa Rule will help you flap your wings. Latinos who grew up in rural areas know that the "newest chicken in the henhouse" always runs and hides to avoid being pecked.

If you grew up under the shadow of domestic violence then you probably make yourself invisible in order to avoid problems and stress. Keep this Chalupa Rule in mind whenever you find yourself in a public setting and get the urge to run to a corner and hide. Don't let emotional ghosts from the past stop your forward motion. No one is going to hurt you anymore. Flap your wings. Crow. You have a *right* to be where you are.

A Lo Largo

We were not going to risk getting pecked. No way. Wings folded and beaks down, these little chickens searched desperately for a place to hide. It could happen anywhere at any time. My sisters and I, and our mom and dad, would walk into a social situation involving people outside of our family circle. The event could have been a V.F.W. bingo in Alice, Texas, a family wedding in Brownsville, or (worse yet) a school event where we had to mingle with people who (gasp) were not even related to us.

At home, just try to shut us up. We were loud, confident, and boisterous. If you came to visit, you would swear all-out warfare had broken out inside. Shouts, yells, and booming voices shook the walls of the small wood-frame home. But that didn't mean a battle or even an argument raged inside. Our family was simply loud, *extremely loud.* Our voices were operatic in our lusty competition for attention.

A bubbling soup of Spanish, English, and Tex-Mex poured out of the house to assault the ear of an unsuspecting stranger. One relative would shout in Spanish, another answer in English, while yet another would serve up an unsolicited opinion in a Tejano mix as tightly wound and intricate as the braids into which *Abuelita* arranged her shiny, black hair. This is the way of Latinos, where family conversation is driven around in fiesta-painted bumper cars of words, shouts, and sentences.

We reveled in exchanges that propelled family folklore, history, and gossip into the next generation of tiny Latinos whose inquisitive ears picked up every word of adult conversation.

Sounds and laughter cemented the family and kept our culture and heritage alive. We carry those memories with us to this day. Our ears still ring with the tickle of jokes, the sobs of tragedy, and even the whispers of secrets that no one in the family dared to utter aloud. The heartbeat of an active, thriving Latino family, these sounds live on and unite us in even the toughest of times.

However, there were many times when silence ruled our lives, when an old aunt's thick, brown finger whipped across stern, pursed lips, turning us into unwilling mutes. No one challenged *Tía's* command for silence.

Why did we fall silent? Perhaps the town doctor had made a house call, seeing to an ailing relative. A house teeming with loud, boisterous Mexicans is not exactly the best environment for a physician to explain medications or outline treatment plans. During those times, utter silence was the order of the day. Back when doctors still made house calls, poor families like ours could not afford to waste even a second of the doctor's time. We stared at his large, black bag filled with medicines, needles, and possible salvation.

We hid in the next room, dying with curiosity and terror. One unsuppressed cough and the doctor might use a sharp needle to inject some *medicina* into our bony, brown behinds.

An older relative always offered the doctor a *cafecito*. There were hushed, urgent negotiations between family members as they corralled dollars and loose change into the sum total of the doctor's fee. Beyond that, only the sounds of a sniffling, bedridden relative dared to break the silence the physician needed in order to do his work. We could not afford to make a single stray sound that could distract the *doctorsito* from his responsibilities.

Talking was also prohibited when an elder spoke, when folktales with a "moral-to-the-story" were told, and when a new visitor endured a "friendly inquisition" by older female relatives. As children, we learned to sniff at the air and pick up signals that would send us into our *silencio, niños* mode.

It was considered polite to be self-effacing. If you hid your own light and tried to act in a sheepish manner then you were acting *como un pollo recién comprado.* Basically, you acted like the newest chicken in the henhouse. The newest chicken always crouched down, keeping a low profile, trying to stay under the radar. You were saying, "Don't look at me. I have nothing to offer. I am too small to be worth your notice. Don't peck at me."

As an adult, I observed that when non-Latinos entered social situations, they walked in heads held high, shoulders back, with their stories, their opinions, and their points of view at the ready. When I was a child there was always a relative around to admonish me by saying, "Keep your opinion to yourself. Even if you're starving to death or dying of thirst, don't ask for anything. Wait until it is offered and if someone says something to offend you, just swallow it."

I don't profess to know why we were raised that way. I am sure it served its purpose in a rural society where visits between distant ranches were few and there was always an air of starchy formality to gatherings. Perhaps it was because, as some family members have told me, there always had to be *respeto*, respect.

At the time, my only concept of public speaking was to eagerly wait for my turn to scream at my cousins during family gatherings. There was always at least a minimum of ten and, at times, up to twenty cousins competing for center stage to tell their stories, or to shout each other down during games of hide-and-seek. We also enjoyed bragging about which of the penny candies we planned to snap up during our sweet-tooth runs to Suzy's *tiendita*. Inside the little store, in the presence of the tiny yet intimidating Suzy, we walked around in hushed reverence, quietly debating the intrinsic value of candy cigarettes, wax bottles of sugary "soda water," and pastel necklaces made of sweet-tart gems.

No expert appraiser at Tiffany in New York matched the intense squint of our eyes as we pushed and shoved each other out of the way, gazing hungrily at the tasty jewels encased in round glass jars topped with "fiesta red" lids.

Our purchases safely stuffed into little brown paper bags,

we exploded onto the dusty *callecita* of Alice, Texas. With our bare feet, we kicked up dusty clouds from the road as we walked to our Tía Elia's house, reverting to loud, boisterous "Tejano talk" we seemed to reserve only for members of our family. Oh, the fights over who had made the best purchase. "*Mira*, mines is more *sabroso* than yours," a cousin would shout. Another would counter with, "I'm gonna wear this candy necklace all day and then eat it after we have Tía Elia's *calabaza con pollo*. Ay, it looks like real jewels, right?"

Throughout these exchanges, our little pack of wandering *Mexicanitos* bound ourselves together with the satisfaction of mission accomplished (we made it through Suzy's without her yelling at us) and with the love/hate/love tumult of cousins who acted more like brothers and sisters than anything else.

All of the camaraderie was abandoned, however, if one of the neighborhood *perros* decided his breakfast of leftover tacos and cheap, dry dog food was not enough. As we tumbled by, I can only imagine the dog viewing us as a feast on the move: cousins-à-la-carte. Hmm, he thought, perhaps a little morsel of *primo* rib will hold him until dinnertime.

This was the one and only time we forgot our relatives' admonishments to remain quiet and unassuming. The threat of attack by a snapping street dog helped us find our voices. We were off, a mongrel of mysterious breed imitating a lion of the African savannah, hunting down a gaggle of screaming cousins. We were crazy with fear as we pounded out a scattered rhythm of panic on the hot, unpaved road. The thick soles of our summer-proof bare feet blurred in flight; our precious *dulces* spilled onto the dirt.

Our screams filled the streets and compelled busybody *señoras* to frown at our cowardice through the patchwork repairs of their screen doors. The dogs rarely bit but always succeeded in propelling our voices into the South Texas stratosphere, full-strength and unrepentant in their ear-shattering volume.

Those screams were nothing compared to the loud, breathless hysterics as we told our tale of horror to aunts and uncles who smiled as they remembered their own "*niño*-hood." Toppling each other in and out of the spotlight, we fought for attention until we experienced at least one or two minutes basking under the full gaze of the *familia*. This was our theater, our homespun vaudeville, a place to express the full range of our emotions.

Somewhere along the way, the turbulence of domestic violence and the periods of desperate poverty lowered the volume of my voice and cloaked my emotions with a shield of protective shyness. *Me hice chiquito.* I made myself small, almost invisible as my self-esteem shrank and my awkward uncertainty grew.

Me hice chiquito. I made myself small when schoolmates talked of luxuries we did not have, like hot running water. *Me hice chiquito.* When, in high school, someone pointed out that the cheap pair of pants I purchased at the discount store "Solo Serve" had a major defect that was only visible in the sunlight. To my shock and embarrassment one of the pants legs was dark brown and the other a lighter shade of brown. I covered up my humiliation with a laugh and a smile and made myself even smaller.

It was also in high school when I had my first opportunity to express myself in a structured, trained manner. Despite my shyness, I was drawn to the Speech and Drama department at McCollum High School. The department was run by a creative, vivacious woman by the name of Ann Dalton. Mrs. Dalton's classes were the first place where I was introduced to the concept of a speech contest. I entered several of them and with her training won some trophies. But it was still there, the overwhelming urge to run and hide. I still acted like the newest chicken in the henhouse.

My first speech contests were an exercise in terror. I was hungry to communicate but too "chicken" to relax. I agonized over the competitions as I perfected my speeches and tried to calm my quivering *plumas*. It didn't help that, on contest day, I faced boys with years of speech training, brand-new clothes, and acres of confidence. Where is that chicken coop when you need it? There was nowhere to hide. It was either flap my wings or wind up with egg on my face.

Time out for a commercial.

Now that I look back at that time in my life, it really is no surprise that my favorite Saturday morning cartoon character was Michigan J. Frog in "One Froggy Evening." Here's the plot: A man discovers a little green frog singing his heart out in the style of Al Jolson. His singing is lusty, open, and loud; full of talent, gusto, and style. The man rushes the frog to talent agents but each and every time, Michigan J. Frog falls silent, quiet as a tomb except for one single froggy croak that reveals none of his hidden abilities. He only sings as loud as Vicente Fernandez or Marc Anthony when no one can hear him. As a matter of fact, there is a Latino version of Michigan J. Frog. He is the little green *Rana* you find on a card from the game of *Lotería*.

In reality, *I* was the Mexican version of Michigan J. Frog. At home I belted out songs, delivered speeches I was practicing for school, and generally expressed myself in a loud, clear voice. Then, when placed in a public setting, this overwhelming feeling of shyness and inadequacy washed over me. It was uncontrollable and seemed impossible to fight. That's when someone in my family dusted off this old Spanish proverb and laid it at my feet: *No seas como pollo recién comprado*. However, in true Tex-Mex fashion, they pronounced the word *comprao*.

I spent much of my childhood in Alice where we had chickens and roosters and turkeys and ducks in the backyard. I was well acquainted with what happens when you introduce a new bird into the henhouse. This *pollo recién comprado* did its best to avoid being "henpecked" by its fellow residents.

Back to the speech contest. That image now once again

fresh in my mind, I realized that in reality no one was going to "peck at me." It was a speech contest, not a henhouse, and I was simply a contestant trying his best. The best that I could do was to walk into the situation with the largest measure of confidence and self-control I could muster.

At that time it wasn't much, but it was enough to signal to the other contestants that, due to my newly discovered self-confidence, I couldn't be "pecked at." I was prepared and could take care of myself. My sophomore year, I placed at the top level of a speech competition. Thank God for family sayings. So, whenever you are in situations that threaten to make you shrink into the "darkest corner of the henhouse" tell yourself this Chalupa Rule: *No seas como pollo recién comprado.* You have an absolute right to be where you are. Feel your sense of belonging. Get comfortable with your surroundings. If you carry these Chalupa Rules and your family love everywhere you go, you will always be home.

In Ann Dalton's speech class, something happened. The floodgates opened and all the years of repressed energy and suppressed thoughts came tumbling out.

With her encouragement and light-hearted approach to coaxing the best out of her students, I began to grow. My self-esteem was still in its *chiquito* mode but there was faint hope that a small *chispa*, a little spark of creativity was there to be developed.

My foray into speech contests helped to raise the volume of my voice and remove the aura of *pollo recién comprado* from my demeanor. One-act play contests. More speech contests. Still more opportunities to speak in front of a group of people and I could feel those feathers fall off me, *poco a poco.*

But it remains a constant struggle for me; there were so many years of "holding back," of staying quiet, that to this day some co-anchors I work with have noticed a tendency I have to trail off at the end of sentences while I am on the air. I will be speaking with strength and confidence. Then, all of a sudden, it appears as if I turn down the volume of my voice, an involuntary reflex. It might be a "ghost" from the past. My voice may contain memories of darker, sadder times when staying quiet and remaining in the background was a way to survive the turbulence in a home where angry voices and raised fists were a weekly and sometimes daily occurrence.

Yes, I have to admit that after more than twenty-five years in the broadcast industry, the *pollo recién comprado* within me is still alive and well and threatening to carry my voice and confidence back to a time when being invisible was the necessary thing to do. This Chalupa Rule is my constant friend and inner "coach." Almost every working day, when the urge to "silence myself" kicks in, this rule comes to my mind.

It has the voice of an older relative, one that carries with it not only love and concern but also more than just a small dose of friendly prodding. I can correct the problem by calling this Chalupa Rule to mind.

No seas como pollo recién comprado, the voice whispers in my ear, urging me to make my thoughts known. "Don't act like the newest chicken in the henhouse," this Chalupa Rule commands as I walk into a room filled with prominent leaders, celebrities, and other well-known public figures.

Perhaps you are already confident. Perhaps you are already a member of the lucky group of people who confidently walk into a large gathering and navigate the intricacies of communication so well that your voice is heard, your thoughts are expressed, and your sentiments are felt. If so, *felicidades*, congratulations to you. If you are not, know that there are others like you who are also working on this issue. I am one of them and I am not ashamed to admit it. So let's flap our wings together and make some noise.

Admittedly, it is very hard to get rid of old habits. As I have mentioned, I still, to this day, struggle to "crow" a little more. Not in a boastful, self-aggrandizing manner but with an approach that radiates a healthy self-esteem. Keep in mind what this Chalupa Rule tells you. When you act like a *pollo recién comprado*, when you make yourself small, *cuando te haces chiquito*, you diminish yourself.

You walk in *already* looking like a loser.

Let your thoughts and your opinions out of that darn chicken coop and into the fresh air. Here is a wake-up call that will get those wings flapping: Latinos are the number one minority in the United States. We have always been here.

We never have been the newest chickens in the henhouse.

Let the magnificent words of Nelson Mandela underscore this Chalupa Rule. On the day of his inauguration he said:

> *Our deepest fear is not that we are inadequate. Our deepest fear is that we are powerful beyond measure. It is our light, not our darkness, that most frightens us. Your playing small doesn't serve the world. There is nothing enlightened about shrinking so that other people won't feel insecure around you . . . and as we let our light shine, we unconsciously give other people permission to do the same.*

Flap your wings. Crow a little. Speak out. Make yourself heard.

No Seas Como Pollo Recién Comprado

Don't Act Like the Newest Chicken in the Henhouse

CHALUPA RULE TWO

2

EL CATRÍN
The Dandy

You Have a Beggar's Body

Tienes Cuerpo de Limosnero

Prontito:

You don't need the newest fashions to do a good job. Gladly accept hand-me-downs. Adjust to the clothes that you have. Fix them up as nice as you can and then get on with the work. It's okay to have a "beggar's body," a body that wears whatever it is given. Wear what you have with pride. Forget about being a fashion plate and concentrate on the job at hand.

A Lo Largo

For six children who grew up in a poor family, new clothes were few and far between. Thankfully, uncles, aunts, and cousins with more money were kind enough to give us their hand-me-downs. Throughout high school and even in college I wore the brightly colored, polyester cast-offs from my Uncle Rosendo. He stood exactly five feet tall. I was five feet, ten inches. Even though the sleeves were much too short for my arms, I wore those shirts to school. You see, I was taught this valuable Chalupa Rule.

Whenever anyone came to the house with bags of used clothing, our parents would tell us, *Recuerden, ustedes tienen cuerpo de limosnero.* We were commanded to have "beggar's bodies." We knew exactly what that meant. No matter the size of the donated clothes, too large or too small, we put them on and adjusted our bodies to make them fit. We learned to have an expandable "beggar's body." Although we always made a game of it, this was serious business. Those were the only clothes we got for a very long time.

But no matter how inexpensive or secondhand my clothes were, I managed to graduate from high school and earn a partial scholarship for college. High school transcripts don't record how stylish your clothes were or the price tag on your shoes. There is no blank space on a college application where you are asked if you wore designer clothing to school every day.

This Chalupa Rule is best illustrated by my experience during my senior year in college. I majored in broadcast journalism and one of the requirements was to produce and videotape a newscast. In the process, we had to take on each of the jobs involved, including anchoring the news.

No problem.

For the taping, I had to wear a business suit.

Big problem.

At the time, the only suit I had to my name was one I had worn (worn out) in high school. It was beige, with wide lapels. It sagged everywhere, exhausted from being worn at every single school function, including the speech competitions in which I participated.

This suit was ready for a garage sale, at best, and definitely not ready for college television. I had no choice. This was the suit I needed to wear because it was the only one I had.

At the time, all of the money I earned from working part-time at Sears and Roebuck and from my substitute teaching job went to groceries, the house payment, and all the other necessities my family needed. There were eight people in the house.

Money was beyond tight and the purchase of a suit was not even within the realm of possibility. As we Tejanos say, *Olvídate.* Roughly translated it means pretty much the same thing as "Fugedaboutit."

The date for the videotaping got closer and closer. Affluent classmates pulled out their designer suits, nice ties, and shiny shoes for this very important project, as a big part of our grade came from the on-camera performance.

My family, wanting me to look my best, desperately searched for an answer. All seemed lost until we made a very special purchase that saved the day.

Gracias a Dios.

I had a brand-new suit to wear for my debut as an "anchorman." Well, not exactly brand-new but to my family's eyes and to my assessment, it was as good as new. The new suit did not cost $500.00. This suit with a new look and a fresh feel did not even cost $150.00. As I can remember, the suit cost exactly twenty-five cents.

Twenty-five cents.

This was a big surprise even to someone like me, who was used to having a *cuerpo de limosnero.* My mother bought a box of orange Rit dye and colored the suit into respectability.

Through quick thinking and resourcefulness, I had a "new" suit to wear. Granted, it was not a designer label. It was not custom-made. It had never been modeled in any fancy fashion show.

It did not matter. The Rit dye transformed the suit into a rust-colored even-toned outfit that I was proud to wear in my very first taping. I wore the suit with confidence. I still have that videotape and every once in a while I dig it out and marvel at my family's creativity under pressure, their ability to make something special out of absolutely nothing.

Again. You can make something special out of absolutely nothing.

There is more to the story. I used that same videotape as my audition for a news reporter position at KSAT 12 in San Antonio. I got the job. My twenty-five-cent Rit dye suit worked just fine.

So, if you have a job interview and don't have the clothes to wear, first:

Ask someone if you can borrow their clothes.
Go to a secondhand store and see what you can afford.
Look through your closet. Wear the best that you have.
Walk in there with your *cuerpo de limosnero* and your self-confidence.

If a twenty-five-cent, rust-colored suit can work for me, a similar "beggar's body" outfit can work for you.

I was many years into my television career before I could afford the appropriate wardrobe for my job as an anchor and reporter. I had to improvise, wearing the same blazers and suits over and over until they absolutely fell apart. I could only afford one pair of shoes at a time and those I wore until they disintegrated beyond repair.

But I realized something. The clothes and shoes don't matter. What is most important? The experience and skill I devel-

oped as a communicator. You can still be presentable in discount clothing and ties purchased from vendors on the street.

To this day, I have a "beggar's body," adjusting myself to fit
into clothes I am given and being creative with a limited
wardrobe.

This Chalupa Rule features *El Catrín*/The Dandy, an image
from Mexican bingo. He is resplendent in his starched finery,
an expensive white tie and tails and a brilliantly polished pair
of shoes. What this rule signifies for me is that you don't need
to be a "dandy," obsessing about fashion and worrying if
someone will notice if your clothes are not the latest designer
wear.

Flash forward to just a few years later when I began work as
a reporter and anchor on New York City television.

I struggled to make it financially in the Big Apple while at
the same time sending a large portion of my money home to
San Antonio. There was no money for new clothes. There was
a demand for stylish, up-to-date clothing for my television
work. What could I possibly do?

Well, I made do with the clothes that I had. When the
shirts fell apart I simply stapled them together or stitched
them at home as best as I could. Taking them to a tailor was
impossible. That cost money and I was told to throw the old,
worn-out shirts away and purchase new ones. Yeah, right.

At work, I sometimes heard, "Mario take off your coat. It's
summer and you must be burning up." I always answered that
I was "just fine" and left it at that. Shoes? No problem. One
sturdy pair of black shoes will do just fine. That is still my practice. One pair of nice black shoes will see you through your
job. If they begin to fall apart, take them to the shoe shop and
get them spiffed up. They can last you up to another year.

No money for new suits? Invest, if you can, in a few nice but
inexpensive ties. What I learned is the following paradox
(thankfully). If you buy a new suit, nobody notices. If you
wear a new tie people usually say, "Wow. Is that a new suit?"

We need to ignore the bombardment of ads for the latest clothing and the newest fad. This was very difficult to do when I first arrived in New York City.

There I was, strapped for cash, needing nice clothes for work and surrounded, absolutely surrounded, by the most elite, exclusive men's clothing stores in the world. We are all human and temptation is hard to fight.

Yes, I walked into those stores, admired the clothes and practically passed out on the floor when I looked at the price tags. Making a polite but quick exit, I hit the streets looking for ways to purchase new clothes on a very tight, almost non-existent budget. All of the expensive-sounding names of the boutiques and department stores proved very intimidating. Until I figured out this important rule in life: the easier the name is to pronounce, the more affordable the clothes. Sears. JCPenney. Target. Get it?

Hence this motto that fits this Chalupa Rule perfectly: "If I can't pronounce it, I can't afford it."

I carefully rotate the clothes that I have and appreciate the value of one dark-blue blazer and a pair of gray pants. They can be worn almost year-round and, if you are careful, can last a very long time. When something wears out, I replace it. That's it. No more.

I appeared on a television show where the wardrobe was provided. I was given an eleven-hundred-dollar John Varvados designer suit. The most beautiful suit I have ever worn, dove gray with pinstripes.

But I couldn't bring myself to keep the suit. It didn't belong to me somehow. That suit, I felt, belonged to someone who needed a second chance in life. I wanted to pass on my good fortune. I didn't want someone else to have a Rit dye experience.

I found an organization in New York City called Career Gear. It provides secondhand suits to men who graduate from job-training programs. A few days before their first job interview, they are referred to Career Gear. This amazing organization outfits the job applicant with the clothing necessary to land a job and insure their future. That's where this designer suit belongs, I decided. Somewhere out there is a guy who wore a thousand-dollar suit to his very first professional job interview. I am sure he wore it well and got the job.

Gary Field, founder and executive director of Career Gear, says this Chalupa Rule fits into their philosophy:

A suit, whether it's used or new, is like a suit of armor. Like a football player doesn't go out on the field without his helmet or without his uniform; like that football player or knight fighting a battle, you need to be strong and feel confident. You can do that with something someone has given you or something new. Oftentimes people let false pride get in the way of so many things. If you open yourself up, people will come your way.

People will help and take care of you but you have to be open to that. But, you have to be able to give back when you're able to.

To me, the rust-colored suit I wore for my first television taping is as valuable as the designer suit. It cost only twenty-five cents but it is worth a million dollars in life lessons: having a beggar's body and wearing what you have can be the richest wardrobe of all.

Don't be a *catrín*/dandy. Have a beggar's body and get to work instead.

Tienes Cuerpo de Limosnero

You Have a Beggar's Body

EL SOL
The Sun

LA LUNA
The Moon

Light of the Street, Darkness of the Home

Candil de la Calle, Oscuridad de la Casa

Prontito:

While traveling on the road to your career, remember to take your family with you. If you are going to get out of poverty, abuse, and discrimination, get out together. Reach back and help them move forward as well. Put time, money, and love into your family first. Shed your light on your own home and *then* try to impress the world.

A Lo Largo

This old proverb is the Latino take on "Charity begins at home." This traditional saying always made me shrink to the size of a postage stamp every time I heard it. When uttered by a Latino parent, it carries the weight of a thousand atomic bombs. It means that you care more for and pay more attention to your friends and others you meet in the street than those who live in your home. You shed sunlight on your friends but only pale, weak moonlight on your own home. This *dicho* teaches me a very important lesson, one that I carry with me to this very day. Take a good look at both of the Chalupa images and read on.

One of my most shameful moments:

I attended college at Trinity University in San Antonio, Texas. One semester, there was money left over from my financial aid package. Since I had very few clothes to my name and most of those were old and worn out, I had a bright idea. I headed straight for a discount clothing store where I knew I could stock up on pants and shirts at affordable prices. The money in my pocket and the racks of (to me) beautiful clothes sent me into my first-ever frenzy of shopping.

About an hour later, I arrived home with several pairs of pants and some shirts as well. I was excited about my purchases and was anxious to show them off to my family.

However, I had an ulterior motive. I attended an expensive university and just about all of the students came from wealthy families. I was one of the few minority students on financial aid. For once, I thought, I could show those rich kids how well a San Antonio guy could dress when there are a few extra dollars in the house.

But no sooner had I stepped through the front door of the house than a disturbing realization hit me. During my shopping frenzy, I had not given a moment's thought to the fact that my sisters were also in desperate need of clothes as well.

The only thought on my mind was to impress my fellow college students.

That thought entered my mind at the exact time I burst through the door, holding my prized shopping bags aloft. I found my five sisters and my mother sitting in the living room watching the inexpensive black-and-white television set that we rented for a few dollars a week. I will never forget the look in their eyes as they watched me enter the house. Hoping to salvage at least one moment of excitement, I pulled out a pair of pants and held them up in front of them. Their faces said it all: excitement for me and a longing to have new clothes of their own.

I had sacrificed the opportunity to share the clothing money with my sisters for a few moments of showing off at school. I lost all interest in the clothes; they seemed heavy and awkward in my hands as I sheepishly stuffed them back into the bags.

To make matters worse, the store where I bought them didn't give refunds or accept returns.

In order to bask in the light and acceptance of fellow college students I had shed no light on my own family. *Candil de la calle, oscuridad de la casa.* You are the light of the street but darkness of your own home.

This Chalupa Rule is an extremely important one in my family. We are always told to share our good fortune with each other and to share in shouldering the pain of sorrow as well.

Early in my television career, I was selected to co-host San Antonio's local version of a national television show called *PM Magazine.* This wonderful opportunity gave me several firsts in my life. It was the first time I ever flew on an airplane, the first time I stayed in a luxury hotel, and the first time I traveled to such exciting places as Europe, Latin America, and Hawaii.

These trips were hard work but they were also exciting and eye-opening. I would try to enjoy myself and many times I did.

However, I could never let go of the fact that, despite the beauty of the locations and the glamour of the first-class travel and accommodations, my family was not with me.

We always like to joke that, as a family, we go everywhere in "lumps"; *el monton*, as we like to say. We crowd into restaurants, fill an entire row of movie theater seats, and fill cars and vans to their utmost capacity. During those working trips while taping segments for *PM Magazine*, I felt an empty space inside. I wanted to share these experiences with my family.

I felt so sad and low that one of our executive producers, the late Jim Pipkin, used to call my quiet, reflective moods "Mario's Blue Funk." I couldn't help it. I sailed the Caribbean in a top-level luxury liner while my family and I lived in an FHA 235 government home. It didn't seem fair to them.

So, I designed a way to try to include my family in these trips. First, everywhere I traveled I collected gifts: souvenirs, jewelry, and t-shirts. It got to the point where I would take an empty bag or suitcase just to accommodate my family's goodies.

Then there were the postcards, written from every location that I visited. One time, I even sent a giant coconut from Hawaii. No box. No wrapping. Just a huge painted coconut with an address label. There was one small problem. There are so many of us that there just wasn't enough room to fit everyone's name on the shipping label. I had to come up with a way to include everyone. No one could be left out. The solution lives in my family to this day. The mailman delivered this coconut to my family simply addressed to: "My Favorite Mexicans."

These sign-ons and sign-offs have evolved through the years and have become "MFM" and "YFM." This way, my entire family is included in the hellos and good-byes. All gifts, all flowers, and all of the "junk food" baskets that I have delivered to my nieces and nephews on the occasion of good grades, birthdays, or just to say "I Love You" carry the short, but weighty, message, "We love you very much, YFM." "Your Favorite Mexicans."

Shed light on your own home before illuminating the street outside. Share your knowledge, your experiences, and your bounty with your family first. But be prepared for criticism. Believe me, I have heard it all. "Get a life of your own." "You should have your sports car, your great apartment, and your nice clothes; take care of that first." And even this rude and outrageous "advice," "Sell your house and let your family members take care of themselves."

It is amazing to me how some people, in the guise of giving advice and trying to help, trample on the very heart of a family. At first, whenever I heard comments like that, I was shocked into stunned silence.

While there are other, more "colorful" ways to tell a person that your life is your own, I developed my own technique for responding to those types of questions. I respond, "This *is* a 'life of my own.' This is the life that I have *chosen*. It is rewarding and fulfilling to help my family. Rest assured that I make time for myself and take care of my needs as well. But again, I repeat, this is a 'life of my own.'"

There's more. I always add, "My family helps me, they love and support me as well. We are very happy with this arrangement. It's what makes our family special."

MFM. My favorite Mexicans. The exchange of love and support continues to this very day. We love to shine the light on each other and then venture out and share it with the rest of the world; not the other way around. That is the order of our little "Mexican Universe."

It is not always *facil*. Putting this Chalupa Rule into practice can be far from easy but the rewards of doing so are great.

I have lived in New York City for over eleven years. During that time I made sure my family also experienced all of the beauty, culture, and wonders of *La Gran Manzana*. But getting several people to New York several times a year for visits proved to be very tough when you have a tight budget. So, other things had to go. Nights out. New clothes. Entertainment. *Pa' fuera*. They were "outta there."

Yes, you can shed light on your family in so many ways. And some of these ways can cost *ni un solo centavo*. For not even a single penny you can write a note of encouragement to your sister or brother and leave it on their schoolbooks.

Thank your mom, dad, or caregiver for a nice dinner. Spend time helping your little sister with her homework before going out for the evening.

Call a lonely *abuelita* on days other than her birthday. In this manner, you shed light on your family, a light of love and good thoughts that are expressed every day and not just dusted off for special occasions.

Do you spend more money on a car that you show off to your friends rather than buy your brother or sister school supplies? Do you spend more evenings with your friends rather than stay home with your children? Are you nicer, more understanding and patient with your friends than with your own family? If so, you are not living in the spirit of this Chalupa Rule.

I will never forget the sting of regret when I broke this rule. I try to avoid the same feeling by doing my best to live up to its values and ideals. Learn this Chalupa Rule and carry it in your *corazón* every day. Take a long, hard look at both of the images, the sun and the moon. Use the sun to shed light on your family; the pale light of the moon is not enough. **Begin the caring and nurturing process at home.**

No Seas Candil de la Calle, Oscuridad de la Casa

Don't Be the Light of the Street, but the Darkness of Your Own Home

CHALUPA RULE FOUR

4

EL DIABLITO
The Devil

The Devil Never Sleeps

El Diablo Nunca Duerme

Prontito:

There are plenty of "little devils" in the world: jealous people who try to cut you down with biting comments and backstabbing. *Let* them talk until they are blue in the face. If you react, if you show emotion, then it's "mission accomplished" for them. Let them lose sleep making shady plans.

It doesn't matter if you never let 'em see you sweat. Beware, though, of another "little devil." This one lives inside of you. This devil is your own worst critic, cutting you down, insulting you, telling you that you are not worth much. Silence that toxic voice, the "mean boss" in your head. Fire him. Retire him. Send him away on a permanent vacation. Do not be meaner to yourself than anyone else could possibly be.

A Lo Largo

This *dicho* is designed to make you behave, to toe the line. It means the devil is always awake and ready to tempt you into trouble of one kind or another.

It also means that there are dangers out there in the big, bad world and while you may be naïve and unsuspecting, the "devil" (however you interpret the devil to be) never closes his eyes and passes up an opportunity to harm you or lead you down the wrong path.

There are other aspects to this Chalupa Rule that can play a role as you try to carve out your life and career. You may be doing the best work you possibly can while at the same time a coworker criticizes everything you do. You may not be bothering a soul in school, keeping to yourself, doing your work, but nevertheless someone is trying to make trouble with you.

In these instances, the "devil never sleeps." *El diablo*, in this case, is the devil of criticism, of backstabbing, and of trying to sabotage others' best intentions. This devil is not going to magically go away. There is always going to be someone jealous of you, threatened by you, or simply annoyed by your very presence.

A veces, así es el mundo. Sometimes, that is the way of the world.

What *can* go away are the toxic ways of dealing with these *diablos que nunca duermen.* Here is what I mean by toxic ways: Whenever we learn that someone is prodding their pitchfork of criticism, negative remarks, and ill will into our sides, it is only human to feel the pain and sting of the attack. However, we must realize that the hurt and anger are only internal reactions. No one else is feeling that anger, that *coraje.*

We are the ones who mope around the house, work, or school, *heridos;* the walking wounded so to speak. The little devils never feel a thing. They have won. Their pitchfork finds a soft, vulnerable spot in our self-esteem and succeeds in low-ering our assessment of ourselves and our work. If we allow those feelings of hurt and defeat to take over our thoughts then it affects everything we do. For those little *diablitos* it is "mission accomplished." If you respond with counterattacks and insults, you lower yourself to the level of the attacker. It will be an endless cycle of "Well, let me tell you something" that has no end. In my opinion, whether they realize it or not, those *diablitos que nunca duermen* are trying to stop you in the tracks of your progress, your movement *adelante*.

So, when you let hurtful comments and harsh "behind-the-back" *comentarios* get to you, that is it, game over. You have stopped moving forward.

Once they know that they have gotten to you, those *diablitos* will take aim with their pitchforks once again and aim for another soft spot. The best response, in my experience, is to "Never let 'em see you sweat."

Recuerda. Haz memoria. Remember. Memorize this.

Once you stop and listen to what people say, you freeze your forward motion. *Sigue adelante. No pares.* Continue forward. Don't stop.

I learned through my own painful experience that there is another *diablo que nunca duerme*. Unfortunately, this one lives inside of us. The *diablo* in the traditional game of Chalupa is bright red, with a long, curling tail, a mocking grin, and a sharp pitchfork. Now picture this bothersome creature inside your head every single day and night. He never sleeps because he is always thinking of ways to torment you.

I am not talking about temptation or ways to make you sin. No, this *diablito* has another sinister purpose. He wants to cut you down and poke holes in your self-esteem until there is nothing left. We allow ourselves to make the meanest, harshest comments about ourselves, more vicious and damaging than any other person in the world could possibly throw at us.

I'm too fat.

I'm ugly.

These jeans look terrible.

I do a lousy job.

No one likes me.

I am not interesting.

If someone talks to us like that we come out fighting. We don't even make a fuss when we tell ourselves such hateful things.

Day in and day out, we collect toxic comments dished out by our very own *diablito.* He never sleeps and never stops creating new ways to cut us down. He is meaner and nastier than any real-life boss we've ever had. But did you know that you can fire him? Give her "walking papers"?

I learned the hard way. After years of doing this to myself, it finally hit me. Why do I allow this to happen? Why do I tolerate this bad treatment, a beating that I generate every day?

I was my own worst enemy; the boss inside of me had horns, *cuernos* that were bigger, sharper, and more devastatingly cruel than any real boss I have ever had.

And I allowed it to happen. *El diablo que nunca duerme* took up residence inside of me, with my permission. He didn't pay rent. He didn't cook *el desayuno.* He never took out the trash. No, he just dumped it on my head.

"Mario, you're not good enough for the job you are doing."

"Mario, who do you think you are; a Mexicano can't anchor the news in New York City."

"You grew up poor and disadvantaged. You have no business educating yourself at a fancy college."

For years, I let him go on and on. Cutting me down. Making me feel small. Diminishing the power of my dreams.

Frankly, it was only through intense therapy that I reached the insight that led to the creation of this Chalupa Rule. The therapy came in the wake of a terrible disaster, the attacks on the World Trade Center. As a reporter, I covered this devastating event and suffered from the emotional trauma and damaging aftereffects of the tragedy.

The need to heal took me to Dr. Barbara Grande, an insightful and perceptive Manhattan therapist who is still working with me on the recovery process.

However, along the way, we made discoveries into other facets of my personality. Therapy revealed the presence of the unwelcome "roommate" I carried around in my head.

So, how do we hand the nasty denizen of this Chalupa Rule his termination papers? Is there such a thing as an eviction notice for a manner of thinking so damaging to our self-esteem?

I came up with my own way. At first, I was embarrassed to reveal it to Dr. Grande so I kept it to myself for a while. Finally, I revealed the process that I had developed for dealing with my demon.

I realized that he was not my "boss." He was a worker in my employ and I no longer wanted him on my payroll. This seems unusual but it worked for me and received Dr. Grande's wholehearted approval. I took this master of *maldades*, this "master of misdeeds," and retired him. I silenced his voice forever.

Believe it or not, in my head I envisioned a gold watch and a complete retirement ceremony. I said to this undesirable employee, "You've put in your years of service. At times, you've even been helpful by teaching me to do positive, critical appraisals of myself. Unfortunately, many times you went too far and damaged my self-esteem. So, here is your gold watch. Go into retirement. I don't need you anymore."

I sent him, his hurtful words, and his painful *cuernos* on his way into the sunset, far away from me.

Without his pitchfork of negative criticism prodding at me every day, I began to feel better about myself. No longer was this *jefe malo*, this nasty boss, tormenting me at home or at work. I silenced this little devil forever.

The devil may never sleep but at least now he is doing it on his own time.

El Diablo Nunca Duerme

The Devil Never Sleeps

CHALUPA RULE FIVE

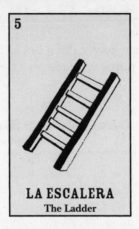

5

LA ESCALERA
The Ladder

The Color of My Skin Is Not a Barrier. It's an Advantage

El Color de Mi Piel No Es Barrera. Es Ventaja

Prontito:

Words are extremely powerful engines that can lead us upward or drive our self-esteem into the ground. Saying someone "broke the color barrier" implies their own ethnicity is an obstacle to overcome. Their skin color is just fine. The problem is racism.

If someone says you are "too sensitive" to racial issues then tell them, "That's why they invented the word 'sensitive,' so that I can use it. Yes, I *am* sensitive. Calling me that won't scare me away from addressing others' problems with racial identity." Your skin color, your ethnicity, is not a barrier. It represents a ladder of culture, beauty, and pride that can lead upward.

A Lo Largo

This is one of my "handcrafted" Chalupa Rules. It was born out of several experiences in my life that put the focus directly on who I am as a Latino, as a brown-skinned person trying to make my way through the United States' working environment.

When I was first starting out in broadcast journalism there were not very many Latinos in the business either in front of or behind the camera. It became the self-appointed task of some people to "decide" where I would best "fit in."

One assessment of my "chances" went as follows: "Since you're Mexican you would do better if you worked in a city where there a lot of other Mexicans."

That is called "pigeon-holing." I am extremely proud to be Chicano and carry that heritage with me everywhere I go. However, I feel that a person's professional ability should translate to any city in the country.

The deeper message this statement conveys is that my skin color is somehow a handicap, a liability I should take into consideration before applying for a job anywhere.

When I was in college the thought of being a news anchor in New York City, of all places, was not even on my radar screen.

The thought of a Chicano from San Antonio, Texas, getting a job in the number one television market seemed inconceivable to me. I had somehow "bought into" the idea, however wrong, that my skin color and my ethnicity were barriers in the advancement of my career. In my years as a broadcast journalist, I have heard it all, including this gem: "Two Latinos should never be anchoring on television at the same time." I protested that comment and realized that, despite years of advancement in civil rights, misperceptions about race and skin color are, unfortunately, very much alive.

Sometimes, as we try to climb *la escalera*, the ladder of our career paths, we hear things that threaten to stop our climb or knock us completely off the ladder.

One that I have heard is: "You don't look Mexican."

Is that supposed to make me feel better? "Whew. Thank goodness. I was worried."

As if being Mexican is something of which I should be ashamed. First, I am not sure what that comment means. I survey my family and see *un arco iris*, a rainbow of colors that represent all the "flavors" of the Latino people. Some relatives are blonde and blue-eyed, some have dark brown eyes and chocolate skin, and the rest are all the shades in between. We are all Latinos. We don't need to be told, "You don't look Mexican or Ecuadorian or Guatemalan" or whatever group is mentioned in this toxic phrase.

"You don't look Mexican" makes me think the speaker has a preconceived stereotype of how a Latino should look. The comment always gets my immediate and firm response: "That is *not* a compliment. I am glad to be who I am and that I reflect one of the many ways a Latina or Latino can look."

But sometimes you can address issues of race and color with a light touch. My little nephew, Maximilian Alberto Pittman, asked me one time why he and I are brown and not white like his brother and cousins. I simply told him, "Max, that's because we have sunglasses all over our bodies." When he is older, he will learn of his Native American, Mexican, and Anglo-American history. I am sure he and his brother Mitchell will be proud.

All through the years, I heard that certain public figures had "broken the color barrier" in order to succeed in their particular field. Along with all of my fellow Americans, I accepted the phrase without question. That phrase, heard in numerous broadcast reports and read countless times in newspaper and magazine articles, played a great role in leading me to think that my skin color was this much-written-about, dreaded "barrier."

"Breaking the color barrier."

Rompiendo la barrera del color.

We hear the words and never stop to question what they are saying. I was the exact same way. Until tennis star Althea Gibson died. Althea Gibson was the first black player to win the U.S. Nationals and Wimbledon. She is legend in the world of sports and continues to inspire people with her story of achievement. When Gibson died in September 2003, news reports were full of her life story that included mention of her many incredible accomplishments. Many of those reports talked of Althea Gibson "breaking the color barrier."

I was among the countless newscasters who repeated that phrase in the days after her death, as we told the world her story. Then it hit me, the realization that the concept is not phrased correctly. In my opinion, Althea Gibson did not break a "color barrier." Her skin color was not the barrier. The barrier was racism. The barrier was bigotry. The barrier was discrimination.

When we call skin color a "barrier" we are investing some very negative connotations on a person's ethnicity. We are in effect saying, "Your color is holding you back. The barrier that is stopping you is a part of who you are, an inextricable, unchangeable part of your being."

No way. Saying that someone "breaks the color barrier" does a tremendous disservice to millions of people of color. My skin color is not a barrier. Althea Gibson's skin color was fine then. Your skin color is fine now.

The barrier was and is racism. That is the obstacle we need to overcome.

That was the birth of this Chalupa Rule. It is time we reverse words and take apart some often-used terms and replace them with thoughts that correctly tell the story.

Words and phrases are very powerful. We must choose them carefully.

I mentioned my thoughts regarding Ms. Gibson to news management at WCBS Television in New York where I work. They agreed with my interpretation. The next time I reported on Althea Gibson, I changed the phrase to say, "Althea Gibson broke through the barrier of racism." That reinstates her skin color and mine to the place where it belongs: as something to be proud of, to be respected. It is not, in any way, something to be considered a stumbling block or obstacle.

Speaking at a public event in Harlem, I brought up my thoughts regarding the phrase "breaking the color barrier." On that night my thoughts were met with tremendous applause. That reception gave me a feeling of pride and satisfaction that I had, in some small way, made a contribution to how race and ethnicity are perceived and reported on in this country.

When you bring up issues such as race and color you must be prepared for someone to try to brush you off by saying, "Oh, you're just being too sensitive."

Sometimes being told you are "too sensitive" can sidetrack you from your train of thought, to get you "off the subject" by making you feel that you are overreacting and dwelling on the issue too much.

So, I share with you the response that I use on those occasions.

If someone tells me I am being too sensitive to cultural and racial issues, I respond: "Well, that's why they invented the word 'sensitive,' so that it can be used. Here goes: Yes, I am 'sensitive' to this issue of color and race." Sensitive is a good word; don't be scared away from using it.

You own who you are as a person and as a Latino. If someone wants to pigeonhole you and determine who you are culturally tell them, "I tell you who I am and not the other way around."

Your ethnic "flavor" and your cultural heritage are not barriers. They are important, integral rungs of the ladder as you climb upward in life. *Recuerda.* **Remember.**

No hay barrera de color. There is no color barrier.

El Color de Mi Piel No Es Barrera. Es Ventaja

The Color of My Skin Is Not a Barrier. It's an Advantage

CHALUPA RULE SIX

6

LA SIRENA
The Mermaid

Swim in Your Culture

Nada en Tu Cultura

Prontito:

Dress up your entire life in the colors and textures of your culture. Speak perfect English and perfect Spanish. But, if you want, have fun with the dialects and accents of your *gente*. They belong to you. Your Spanish accent, if you have one, is okay. You are right. Others' perceptions of you are wrong. Swim in your culture. Show it off to the world.

A Lo Largo

Although this Chalupa card, with its voluptuous *Sirena/*
Mermaid, always brought out giggles and mischievous smiles
in us when we played the game as children, it also carries im-
portant significance for those of us who try to navigate the
United States with our bicultural legacy. This is my original
Chalupa Rule.

La Sirena is a creature of both the air and water. She goes
through life navigating both elements with ease. To me, this
beautiful mermaid represents Latinos living in the United
States who must cope with life here while preserving their *heren-*
cias. Like *La Sirena,* Latinos must learn to swim in both cultures.

So many times in life, I felt "half-in and half-out" of the cultural waters when it came to embracing the "Mexican" in me.

I grew up in South Texas a fourth-generation Mexican
American. On one hand I had people from Mexico telling me
I wasn't a "real Mexican" while on the other many in the
United States devalued my U.S. citizenship by trying to ma-
roon me on some island of indeterminate ethnicity. I went
through some of the typical stages that many U.S. Latinos experience. In my early years I said I was Spanish. Later, I iden-
tified as Hispanic and/or Latino while always keeping a close
eye on those with whom I was speaking, trying to gauge their
reaction, desperate for their approval.

Now, I swim in my culture. *I* decide who I am and not the
other way around. I declare and proclaim my Native American blood, the hints of possible Sephardic Jewish heritage,
the touch of Irish, and of course the rich Mexicano cultural
history. For so many years, I allowed others to tell me who and
what I am.

I am proud to tell people that my New York apartment
looks like a "mariachi threw up in it" with its tangerine
kitchen, bright yellow dining area, riot of plants, and Mexican
masks. It reflects exactly who I am.

This Chalupa Rule, *La Sirena*/The Mermaid, is a challenge to you. Learn about your culture, your family, your heritage. Then, stop swimming half-in and half-out of the cultural waters. Swim entirely in your culture; it will make you a richer and infinitely more interesting U.S. citizen.

I used to try to "fix" my Spanish whenever I was around other people from other areas and countries whose Spanish I felt was "better" that mine. I would do some language housekeeping and sweep "Tejano-flavored" words under the rug. Out comes the dust pan and into it I dump phrases like *órale* and *vato* that I feel are not "proper" Spanish. *Órale* means, "Hey now" and *vato* means "dude." They are fun Tex-Mex words of which I became ashamed.

I even became someone else. Automatically, I erased generations of my proud South Texas heritage and put on an accent and manner of speaking that was and is not "me." It is a certainty that those other Latinos I was speaking with picked up on the artificiality of my speech. It didn't seem to matter to me. I felt I was speaking "proper" or, as some people say, "Spain" Spanish.

I learned that even in Spain there are different dialects, accents, and regionalisms. It suddenly dawned on me that I kept performing "Mexican Makeovers" on my language in order to feel accepted.

Regionalisms and dialects are unique and valid in the areas where they developed. In my opinion, we as Latinos should in no way look down upon others' ways of speaking Spanish. Their dialect belongs to them and to the generations of Latinos who came before them. Their particular phrases and flavors are little "museums" of heritage that we should respect and acknowledge.

Yes, I have my general Spanish that I use in my daily transactions with fellow Latinos from other parts of the United States and Latin America. However, no longer do I "exorcise" my flavor, my particular words. They are "me."

When I finally relaxed and allowed my Tex-Mex–flavored Spanish to shine through in conversation, the response was immediate and overall very positive. People could pick up on the fact that I was being "real" and, by speaking in my usual accent and regionalism, was being true to who I am and where I come from.

Granted, there will always be someone who will look down their nose at an accent, at a variation in what they believe to be the "correct" Spanish. If they become insistent, then do what I always in a situation such as that one. Speak out.

Remember Chalupa Rule Number One: *No seas como pollo recién comprado.* Don't act like "the newest chicken in the henhouse." Flap your wings and in a polite but firm voice say, "This is my Spanish. It's mine. I own it. This dialect is correct for me."

With all of this said and done, I feel it is vital for Latinos and everyone else to take Spanish class, to learn the history of the language, its grammar, and how it developed in the various cultures of Spanish-speaking regions around the world. If you choose to speak in what is generally termed as correct Spanish, then *adelante*, go for it. I have three languages. I proudly tell people I speak English, Spanish, and Tex-Mex. My three languages.

You can swim in your culture in hundreds of different ways. Some of them are as simple as what you name your cat or dog. Naming your pet with something that carries cultural flavor from your Latino background also tells your children that you are proud of your heritage. "Spot" or "Lucky" are cute names if that's what you're looking for but give it some thought and make your four-legged friend a true member of the *familia.*

But perhaps, when it comes to this Chalupa Rule, I've gone a little too far. I had a dog, a thirteen-year-old, four-toothed Chihuahua that I adopted from the Humane Society of New York. I figured we're a perfect match. We were both older, missing at least one tooth, and Mexican. Perfect.

Then it came time to name him. True to the spirit of this Chalupa Rule, I bestowed upon my Mexican friend the most ethnic name I could conjure up.

His name: *Popocateptl Tlaloc Cuautemoc Quetzalcoatl Huitzilopochtli Paricutin Cutirinicuaro Bósquez Alcalá the Third.* Try to say it. It goes something like this: *Popocateptltlaloccuautemocquetzalcoatlhuitzilopochtliparicutincutirinicuarobósquezalcalathethird.* People are stunned at the fact I can actually say this name over and over without stumbling. If we ever meet, try me.

I called him "Huitzi" for short. It's pronounced *Weé-tsee* and it is short for *Huitzilopochtli,* the Aztec god of war. He may have had only four teeth, but he could still have a tough name.

Here is my reasoning for giving Huitzi his mile-long name: Those fancy A.K.C. *perros* can have long, intricate names that run on for miles. I figured a homeless Mexican street dog has the same right to a long, fancy name. And to boot, he had powerful Aztec gods to protect him.

He needed the help. Huitzi had cancer, a collapsed trachea, and an open heart valve. But thanks to the Humane Society of New York and the Aztec gods, he lived a long life.

He is an example of how I learned to swim in my culture. I proudly announced his name on television and everyone learned to pronounce at least a shortened version of his tongue-twister name.

Underneath the silliness of this story, even though every word is true, is the underlying message that I send my nieces and nephews and anyone who cares to listen: even your pets can carry your cultural flavor. It gives a "green light" to others, that they, too, can infuse culture in all aspects of their lives.

The only problem is that I couldn't fit poor Huitzi's entire name on his dog tag.

Sometimes life will take you far away from the physical roots of your culture. You may move to another city, another state, or a different country. That situation poses a special challenge. How you can swim in your ethnicity when you are completely out of your cultural waters? Lisa Quiroz, former publisher of *People en Español* magazine and current vice-president of corporate responsibility for Time Warner, knows what that is like. This proud Puerto Rican-Mexican leader finds ways to connect with her culture.

> *All my life being a Latina has been a source of strength, pride, inspiration, and connection. As a little girl growing up in a white working class suburb of New York City I was often the only Latina in school, on teams, in clubs, and on my block, but my family instilled such a deep sense of culture, history, and pride in who I am that I never felt left out or different—I was special. "You come from a rich, proud history," my grandmother often told me as she listened to her Mexican music and made* pollo en mole. *She made sure that I was raised with that culture and history. Every time Tony Aguilar came to Madison Square Garden, there we would be watching his famous "ranchero" show.*
>
> *If the Ballet Folklorico made a rare appearance in New York City we would be first on line to buy tickets. When I was eleven she took me to Mexico for the entire summer break. What a wonder! We traveled by bus to over ten cities, climbed pyramids, ate tacos from the street, and listened to live mariachis playing all the songs I grew up hearing. The trip changed me forever. Now, as an adult, I have had the chance to foster that sense of pride and community by launching the best-selling Hispanic magazine in the country,* People en Español, *and now I can contribute to ensuring that all Latinos can raise their children with the same pride, cultural knowledge, and strength that were given to me by my grandmother—a strength uniquely American and Mexican.*

This Chalupa Rule, "Swim in your culture," does not promise that the waters will always be calm. As we say in South

Texas street Spanish, *Ponte aguila*. Basically, it means you need to be eagle-eyed and ready to deal with issues that arise when you proudly display your culture. One time, when I used my Tex-Mex accent on television, a producer approached me, wondering if it was appropriate for me to speak that way on the air. My response? It's my accent. I own it. I am proud of it.

If I had used an Italian, French, or Irish accent, I am sure no comment would have been made. Instead people usually say, "How romantic. How sexy. How sophisticated." Our accents deserve the same regard. For some reason, the accent I used made that person uncomfortable. That's for them and their therapist to figure out. I am doing just fine with my "flavor."

It's time for people to *get* comfortable with it. I speak clear, correct English. I speak clear, correct Spanish. In addition I speak clear, correct "Tex-Mex." So, remember, swim in your culture. If you have your regional flavor, your local dialect, and you want to speak that one as well I say go for it; *éntrale*.

It's all a matter of perception. Your accent is correct. Peoples' perception of it is wrong. Your culture is correct. Their perception is wrong. Somehow, some people might perceive our accent, clothing, or regional dialect as something negative, elements of ourselves that we should cloak and hide from the light.

No way. *Para nada*.

Say it loudly. Wear it proudly. Learn your cultural history passionately. You are not the one with the problem; they are. Keep thinking, "I am right; your perception of me is wrong." Let *La Sirena* of this Chalupa Rule teach you how to stay afloat and navigate both worlds. But remember, you have to be comfortable swimming in the water. If you look ill at ease, others will pick up on that negative energy.

Come on in. The cultural waters are fine.

Nada en Tu Cultura

Swim in Your Culture

CHALUPA RULE SEVEN

LA MANO
The Hand

That's Why They Call It "Work"

Por Eso Le Llaman "Trabajo"

Prontito:

A day at work should be just that, a day at work, full of energy, creativity, and dedication to the job. That's why it's not called a "hobby" or "vacation" or "playtime." At the end of the day you should be spent, tired from putting in a good day's work. If you leave work or school completely refreshed and free from the least bit of weariness, then you did not put in all your efforts.

The job is not "yours." It is entrusted to you. You do not own it "forever." Every day at work, you should perform as if it is your first day and your last day on the job, pouring all your dedication and concentration into the tasks at hand.

A Lo Largo

This Chalupa Rule bears the image of *La Mano* because in my family, just about every job an adult ever had involved manual labor. Ever since I can remember, the work of their *manos* supported families, provided for educations, and helped other relatives in need.

Our photo albums include pictures of relatives taking a brief break from picking cotton in order to smile for the camera. The pictures do nothing to depict the searing Texas heat, the stinging insects, and the risk of snake bite. But there they are, young and old alike, working the fields with their hands.

Their hands also held hammers, raised crops, fed chickens, and butchered meat at packing plants. Their *manos* sewed quilts, painted houses, and slapped little balls of dough into tortillas.

My earliest recollections bring to mind hardworking hands stirring steaming pots of bubbling *caldo*; struggling to perform home repairs on old, broken cars; and pulling harsh, thorny weeds from backyard gardens. None of those hands shied away from work. They rose at dawn, worked long hours, and then—calloused, dusty, and exhausted—tried to get some rest at night. No matter what part of Latin America we come from, almost all of our families have hands like the ones that I describe.

Those are the hands that squirreled away dollars and cents so younger hands could push a pen instead of a wheelbarrow, drive a nice car instead of a herd of cattle, and sew stitches into an ailing body instead of into a ragged dress beyond saving.

El trabajo. Work. For my father it began at four o'clock in the morning, when he and my mother would rise to get his lunch and breakfast ready for a seemingly endless workday that lay ahead. For others it started with a dark, shadowy bus ride at dawn, destination: *Gringolandia*, where huge, luxurious houses needed dusting and waxing and primping. Still, for others work began whenever someone needed an odd job performed at wages that barely fed and clothed even one person, let alone an entire family.

That, I remind myself, is work. *Trabajo.*

An education allows you to pursue a dream, chase down a passion, and grab hold of a future. The career it creates for you is still work but, in my opinion, can never compare with the grueling, back-breaking labor those who make possible our education had to endure. It is to your family members and mine, past and present, I look to for inspiration when I think of this, my "handcrafted" Chalupa Rule, "That's why they call it work." It was developed through years of watching my older relatives dive into their work, both on-the-job and at home. Rarely, if ever, did I hear the constant whining and complaining you tend to hear nowadays. I include myself in that observation.

Latinos of the generations before us never hesitated to jump into the task at hand and keep at it until it was done and done perfectly. I am sure there are exceptions to that but I did not see that often. They arrived home, exhausted and hungry and perhaps with a comment or two about how tough their jobs were, but they seemed to realize intuitively what I finally came to realize myself:

Por eso le llaman trabajo. That's why they call it "work."

It is not called recreation or vacation or even a pastime. The word is "work," *trabajo.*

I may sound like a *lambiache*, which means "kiss-up" in Tex-Mex (it may mean something else in other dialects so my apologies), but it is important to remember that you owe your company, your employer, a full day of concentrated effort and dedication, the best performance you can give.

Speaking of giving, I am of the opinion that we take too much for granted when we speak of "my" job, "my" position at work. This may be stating the obvious, but it's important to remember the job is not "ours"; it is not our possession, it does not belong to us "forever." We are entrusted with a role, a responsibility, but it is not ours to keep. We hold it only as long as our employer wishes, as long as the economy can sustain it, or as long as we desire to be there. But it is not "our" job. Your employer doesn't "owe" you the job. You have to earn it every day.

Taking this perspective changes your approach to work. It is a garden that needs tending every day. Here are some "gardening" tools that can help. They are facets of this Chalupa Rule that I developed through my years on the job.

I heard some excellent advice while working in radio as a newscaster and news director. The programming director, Leo Vela, said that when your day is through, if you feel drained and spent, it means you've put energy into your work. If you finish too rested and very relaxed, like you just spent a day at the *playa*, then it's a good indication you haven't put much effort into the job. Every day at work, you should feel the following way: "It's your first and your last day on the job."

Think about it.

When it's your first day at any new job, your concentration level is at an all-time high. You plunge into every task at hand with energy, enthusiasm, and, as we Tejanos say, *ganas*—a desire to work.

When it's your last day on the job, many times you have the feeling that you want to leave everyone with a good impression of your work. You are at your best so that your employer will give you a good recommendation.

Combine those two feelings and live them every day at work. *Por eso le llaman trabajo.*

These elements are very important when it comes to this Chalupa Rule:

1. **Make yourself irreplaceable.** Find ways to make your performance unique, of a different and better quality than how another person might do the same

job. You will be harder to replace because of special energies and skills you invest in the job.

2. **Find your talent.** There are numerous ways we can put our special abilities to work. Your particular "talent" can be as simple as being the most prompt person at work. If that is the case, develop the skill of being the best "arriver-on-timer." Believe me, that talent is rare and will definitely be prized and noticed by your *jefes,* your bosses. In my present job, we are due on the set exactly five minutes before air time. Every morning, I do my best to be there at the exact five-minute mark. Believe me, that "skill" is noticed. I jokingly tell the crew that I may not have a lot of talent, but I definitely am the best "arriver-on-timer" in the business. Again, find your talent, whatever that may be. You will stand out from the crowd.

3. **Have a meeting with yourself.** Give *yourself* a periodic, honest job review. Put yourself in your boss's or teacher's position. What questions would they ask? Has your performance slipped? Are you cutting corners when it comes to quality? Are you bringing personal problems to the workplace? Go ahead, have at least one "meeting with yourself." When it comes time to meet with a supervisor, you will be much better prepared for the experience.

4. **Rededicate yourself to your work.** If you have a meeting with yourself and find that your quality and concentration are lacking, then rededicate yourself to your job. Make it a small yet nice occasion. Have a hot cup of coffee with your favorite *pan de dulce,* and while you're sitting there, eating

your sweet bread and drinking your *café con leche,*
make a pledge to refocus your energies at work in a
positive direction. From that moment forward, after
your "rededication ceremony," you will put into effect all the changes and adjustments to your performance.

My passion for reading shapes my philosophy on work.
Out of the countless books and magazine articles I have read
through the years, some words stand out due to their clarity
and power. Some of those thoughts apply directly to this
Chalupa Rule. They may come from unusual sources but they
still offer valid advice we all should follow. Years and years
ago—and don't even ask my why—I picked up a discount
book titled *The Whole Truth and Nothing But* by Hollywood
columnist Hedda Hopper. I am sure the reason I purchased
this paperback is because it was secondhand and inexpensive.
In the book, I discovered a powerful phrase that I try to in-
corporate into my work ethic. I am not always perfect at doing
so, but I still give it a try.

In her book, the late Ms. Hopper describes a typical day in
the life of a Hollywood movie star. She details the pressure,
the early hours, and the sacrifices a performer makes every
day. But there's more. Ms. Hopper explains how the entire
film crew looks to the actor or actress for cues to their mood,
as that will affect their entire day. She writes:

*Because their moods will be affected by hers, she has to set the
emotional climate for the day—no headaches, heartaches,
or bellyaches for her.*

Every day since I read that passage, I make a sincere attempt to follow the wisdom of those words. Yes, I am human
and so are you, and it's tempting to weigh down your friends,
family, fellow students, or coworkers with *todos tus problemas,*

all your problems. It just feels good sometimes to unload your worries, but remember they have their own.

We all know someone like that. It's all about them. Their sentences all start with "I, I, I" and you're thinking, "*Ay, ay, ay*. There they go again." If you remember these words, "no headaches, heartaches, or bellyaches," then you won't be so tempted to slow the workday down with a pity party in your honor. Keep in mind what the late Ms. Hopper said, people at work look to you for cues on how the day will go. Send the right message: that it's going to be a pleasant, productive day at work.

This next suggestion may seem trivial, not even worthy of mentioning, but I promise you it carries a power of its own.

Every day before you leave your job or your school, leave your work space the way you found it. Put papers back in order, clear the workspace, and prepare it for the next day's work. This means that your office, your desk, your kitchen, your locker at school, wherever you perform your tasks, should really be a "clean slate" at the end of the day.

There is a feeling of satisfaction the next morning when you arrive for work or school and everything is where it belongs, ready for you to access it whenever it is needed.

I give myself permission to be as messy as I want to while working; I feel it's part of the creative process to let go and concentrate only on the job at hand. *Pero*, but, when the work is done everything goes back into place.

Again, you may think it's a small point but I can't tell you how many times people have made positive comments about my little Chalupa Rule.

Y no creas que los jefes no toman nota de esto. And don't think your bosses don't notice this either. Of course they do.

Remember back in school? Even on the very first day of kindergarten or first grade, at the end of the day, the first thing the teacher said was, "Put everything back where you found it; everything goes back into its proper place." That's one of the first rules of professionalism and we forget all about it. *Qué pena*. Shame. Shame. Shame. Those teachers, they know from experience what they are talking about. If they allowed all the students to leave their personal possessions and school items *donde les dé la gana*, wherever they felt like it, then chaos would reign in class.

Somewhere along the way, we forgot the teacher's instruction. So, if you need to, program a little voice in your head that sounds like one of your elementary school teachers and let him or her talk to you when you are finished with your work.

It will serve as a reminder of this Chalupa Rule and as a tribute to all the hardworking teachers out there.

La Mano. The Hand. The image that goes along with this Chalupa Rule symbolizes hard work, dedication, and attention to detail.

When you need money to support your family, explore all possibilities, all avenues of work. But hey, it doesn't have to be boring. You just have to be willing to take some chances. You have to be willing to expand your horizons.

For our large family, money was always in short supply. Even when I had a television job in San Antonio, the echoes and reverberations of a financially deprived childhood carried over into adulthood. I had to look for extra work. I found it where I least expected it.

As a young boy, I would go with a family friend and help clean the houses of the people who lived on the rich side of town.

While carrying a full load of studies in college, I also worked as a "guinea pig" for psychic experiments and had my head shaved for a Vidal Sassoon fashion show.

While working as a radio newscaster, I also threw a paper route with my family, for about thirty-five dollars in grocery money.

While working in local television, I also worked as a singer at Seaworld of Texas. Yes, that was me riding a Shamu float several times a day, singing my heart out. It was all good, honest work, and guess what? The paychecks cashed just the same as any other job. Sometimes you think to yourself, "Oh I couldn't possibly do that job, it's menial, it's beneath me, what will my friends think?"

Pero cuando se necesita dinero, no hay tiempo para poner aires. When you need money, there is no time to put on "airs."

Jump in. Get the job. Do it. Get paid.

For example, I have even performed in a shopping mall's food court, dressed like a polyester cowboy complete with white hat, fringe, *and* a tambourine. This, after having been on television for years. It was a little uncomfortable, looking like a Mexican Roy Rogers while my former television colleagues looked on during the mall's grand opening ceremony. I am sure they wondered if I had lost my mind.

There is no shame in good, honest work. Are you up to the challenge?

Again, the check cashed and I got to help my family with much-needed extra money. Let's say it again, together:

There is no shame in good, honest work.

Okay, I know there are days when you absolutely don't feel like working. You don't have the *ganas,* the desire to do your job. Believe me. I know the feeling. I get up at 3:00 in the morning to go to work.

At any point in the day when I feel my energy and desire to work begin to sag, I call to mind a line from my favorite Woody Allen movie, *Bullets Over Broadway.* In the scene, the gangster's girlfriend is not in the "mood" for hanky panky.

Her maid walks by and says, "Honey, you better *get* in the mood because that's what's paying the rent."

Funny line and very valid.

So, when I overhear a coworker whine and complain about not being in the mood for work I always say,

"You better *get* in the mood because that's
what's paying the rent."

Por Eso Le Llaman "Trabajo"

That's Why They Call It "Work"

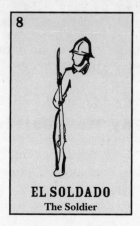

EL SOLDADO
The Soldier

Always Guard Your Little Pile of Beans

Guarda Tus Frijolitos

Prontito:

Resist the urge to divulge everything to everybody. Keep some information to yourself until you know that the person you're speaking with merits your trust. Keep a reserve of caution in everything you do.

A Lo Largo

Híjole, do I have a big mouth sometimes. In Tex-Mex street talk, I am *osicon*, blabber-mouth. Whenever there is even a hint that something good is coming my way, I have to tell the whole world. The whole world.

"Hey, I'm about to go and have lunch with So-and-So. It's about a project I'm working on. The project is about blah-blah-blah." There I go again, spilling all my *frijoles* for everyone to see. Many times, the big project doesn't pan out and I have a glob of *huevo* on my face.

Then there are the times that, before I get to know someone well, I tell them my whole life story, problems and all. Someone asks how much money I make, how much I pay in rent, or my opinion about someone's work performance and sometimes I go for it, again spilling my guts and regretting it later.

And all of this happens because I forget a very important Chalupa Rule: *Guarda tus frijolitos*. Guard your little pile of beans.

I heard this saying often during my childhood. If there was a neighborhood dog that had the reputation of chasing kids down the street, then we would *guardar nuestros frijolitos* whenever we walked by his house.

This saying meant we held back our complete trust, maintaining a reserve of caution when dealing with this situation.

If someone was not completely trusted then you were told *guarda tus frijolitos* around that person until you were certain of their intentions and trust. The message is clear. When you are around that person, if they have not yet earned complete trust, then keep a "little pile of beans" to yourself until you know more about them.

This measure of reserve can serve you well. If you are new on the job and don't completely know everyone yet then *guarda tus frijolitos*; resist the urge to divulge absolutely everything about yourself in order to gain acceptance.

This saying can be useful when you are in situations that cause your little voice of concern to whisper in your ear. Is the place you are in safe? Do the people you are with have the best of intentions? Are those who are listening to your ideas and plans worthy of that information?

If not, then *guarda tus frijolitos*, keep that little pile of beans to yourself. Like the soldier in the Chalupa image, you must guard your safety, question your choice in friends, and exercise good judgment when bringing your innermost dreams and desires into the light.

This Chalupa Rule also advises you that, like the soldier in the game of Mexican bingo, you should carefully guard your storehouse of self-esteem and confidence. These are precious possessions that many times caustic comments from others can erode.

This *dicho* is a familiar friend, thanks to my many relatives who, through the years, sent it my way in the form of counseling and advice. In addition, it's a two-for-the-price-of-one Chalupa Rule.

Here's the first way you can use this Chalupa Rule. If your intuition is whispering in your ear to be on guard about something, listen to it. Trust that inner voice that perhaps is telling you to proceed with caution. Guard your little pile of beans.

In our personal and professional lives, there should always be a reserve of information that you should keep to yourself; despite the temptation, don't tell everybody everything. And, if there is information you know about others and are tempted to share it, *guarda tus frijolitos*/keep it to yourself.

The second way involves your long-range plans. If you have hopes and dreams and feel the person listening may try to downplay your goals then keep them to yourself.

Guarda tus frijolitos.

This can be a simple yet powerful tool in the business world, where the temptation is always there to be the town crier, the one who knows all in the office, the schoolyard, or in the neighborhood.

This *dicho* will remind you that it's best to not always divulge all of your information to everyone.

Have guarded, professional reserve. Watch what you reveal about yourself and especially others.

Guarda Tus Frijolitos

Always Guard Your Little Pile of Beans

CHALUPA RULE NINE

EL MELÓN
The Melon

There Is No Science to It

No Tiene Ciencia

Prontito:

If you look at your future or a large project in one "giant lump," it might seem impossible to achieve. Break the big picture down to its smallest elements. Do those steps one at a time, and slowly the entire dream will emerge. The most advanced technology owes its existence to the tiniest of parts: one bolt, one wire at a time. Do the same with your life. Keep it simple and the biggest of dreams will come true.

A Lo Largo

The translation into English simply does not do this Chalupa Rule justice. To simply say there is no science to it doesn't even begin to do the trick. And yet that phrase, *no tiene ciencia*, has solved many problems in my life.

For example: If you can't afford regular furniture and have to buy the kind that comes in a box in a million pieces that you have to put together yourself, how do you do that? If there is a leaky faucet in the house and there is no money for a plumber, how do you fix it yourself? If a new computer program or system at work stands between you and advancement in your job, how do you learn it? If you dream of a college education, a rewarding career, or a life without domestic violence and abuse, how do you attain it?

¿Es posible? If the mental image of your dream is so huge it barely fits in your head, can you really make it happen?

Well, if you continue to view that dream in actual size—gargantuan, enormous to take in all at once—then probably not. But if you let this Chalupa Rule guide you, the path will be easier to follow. And, although countless Latinos have either said or uttered this proverb, I can thank my Tía Elia for empowering me with its simple, yet profound wisdom.

Like the *tías* of many Latinos, Elia Alcalá, my mother's sister, had the strength, determination, and willpower to run an entire country. She developed those skills while raising her brothers and sisters, including my mother, after her mother died very young. Tía Elia never married and never strayed from her self-appointed duties as head of the house where money was scarce and mouths to feed were many.

The men in the house were self-employed carpenters. The women worked at home and occasionally in the fields. Thoroughly self-sufficient and determined to support themselves they, along with their sister Elia, put food on the table and clothes on their backs.

However, that was about the extent of their financial

reach. If anything fell into disrepair, from dresses to plumbing, it was their responsibility to get it fixed, to get it sewn, to get it running once again. If they didn't know how to do something, they made it their mission to find out. For them, no job was too big. The phrase, "there is no science to it" served to clear away the fog of confusion or perhaps despair that overwhelms you when a seemingly gigantic task is placed before you.

The Chalupa Rule advises you not to be overwhelmed by something when you look at it in its entirety. Slice it up and take it piece by piece. Tía Elia taught me that. She raised me and was my "second mother." She always had the patience to walk me through complicated tasks.

Tía Elia would break huge chores down to the simplest of components, step-by-step. When I couldn't accomplish a task she would always say, *"No tiene ciencia"*/There is no science to it. One bit at a time. If you can handle the tiny steps, you take care of the entire job. This wonderful, resourceful woman helped to raise me when, after my parents' traumatic divorce, we were forced to move back to Alice, Texas, to the family home.

As a small child, happy for her company, I eagerly followed Tía Elia everywhere her busy energy would take her, to feed the chickens, to mow a large lawn with a push mower, to make the simple repairs necessary to run a house on a tight budget. A leaky faucet, a rusty hinge, a dilapidated chicken coop.

Tía Elia always gave me the confidence to achieve things myself. She would hand me the hammer, the screwdriver, and at the same time try to hand me the confidence she knew I would need in life. Immediately, Tía Elia would see a look of confusion cloud my face. How could a little Chicano kid presume to fix a leaky garden faucet?

She always called me "Maro."

"Maro," she would state with the utter confidence of a woman who helped raise ten brothers and sisters. *Maro, no tiene ciencia.*

And that was that. Tía Elia made it her mission to guide me through the process of learning a new task. The phrase *No tiene ciencia* saw me through.

"There is no science to it." Even the largest piece of space shuttle equipment is put together one bolt, one rivet, one sheet of metal at a time. In her basic, no-nonsense way, my Tía Elia knew that. Your *tías* and *tíos* know it as well.

It doesn't have a science. There's no science to it.

Break something big and scary down to its most basic building-blocks, its most basic elements, and it won't be so frightening. As you might imagine from my career and this book, my passion is communication, writing to be specific.

When I was exploring all kinds of avenues that might lead to getting a book published, I searched far and wide for books, magazines, and articles that could lead the way.

One book that I found is *The Sell Your Novel Toolkit* by Elizabeth Lyon, published by Blue Heron books. Ms. Lyon explains various ways to sell a book. She lists several paths to success in publishing.

The ninth way she presents is the most intriguing and the most helpful to this Chalupa Rule.

Here is how: Ms. Lyon's ninth way talks about combining all of the previous eight book-selling techniques she outlined. Those methods included writing letters, setting up meetings, and networking, to name a few. This ninth way includes mention of a fancy, complex-sounding term that is a perfect example of my Chalupa Rule, "There is no science to it." Ms. Lyons introduces a concept called "The Morphogenic Field," a term she says was developed by a scientist named Rupert Sheldrake. Yes, the term "morphogenic field" is a mouthful, but here is the meaning from Ms. Lyon's book:

> . . . *an activated territory that exists in a state of energy. When the field becomes sufficiently energized, it "morphs" from potential into matter.*

Got it? No, I didn't get it the first time either.

Una vez más. One more time. Your ideas, your dreams, your aspirations already exist, but in a nonphysical state. They are one "big picture" on the movie screen of your imagination.

When you take action to make your dream come true, it enters the physical world of reality. Anyway, that is my interpretation of the "morphogenic field." Every little step you take—a phone call to ask questions, a book you buy to find out more, or a night class you take—all add up to make your dream come true.

It begins to "morph" into reality.

All of it bit by bit, *pasito a pasito.* Those little steps turn into the big picture before you know it. What seems to be overwhelming is really a jigsaw puzzle of little pieces that come together to create your dream. There is no science to it. There are only small steps that add up to the big picture. Make that one phone call, ask that one question, read that one article, and before you know it, your dream—fully formed and "ready-to-go"—will come knocking on your door.

Here is a perfect example of how this Chalupa Rule can be illustrated to your children. It's perfect because your *niños* can see it, touch it, and experience it for themselves.

A warning. You may feel like pulling your hair out at times during this project but the effort is well worth a bald spot or two.

Go to a store like Target or Wal-Mart. Purchase an inexpensive piece of "assemble-it-yourself" furniture: a bookcase, a small chest of drawers, or a television stand. It really doesn't matter.

Hopefully, it's something you can use in your home or perhaps give to someone in the family who might need the furniture.

With your child, spread out all the tiny screws, various sizes of shelves, and all the furniture parts.

Pull out the instructions and give them a quick scan; let

them completely overwhelm you. Don't worry, that feeling will come quickly. The both of you will become *desesperados*. How on earth are you going to put this thing together?

Then, start with step number one, reading the instructions with care, taking it all one step at a time.

Gradually, as you proceed with the assembly process, you both will see the furniture become a reality, growing from the mountain of small parts into its final shape. It will "morph" from just an idea into a real, physical object you can see and touch and admire. You did it. The furniture is "standing in" for your goal, your dream, and you just proved to yourselves that they can be "constructed" in much the same way.

When it is over, tell your children: Have faith in the instructions. Make sure all the parts are there. These two steps can apply to anything you do in life, by the way. Have total, absolute faith in the steps you need to take to make your dream come true. Make sure all the parts are there: the training, the education, and the hard work.

Keep repeating this Chalupa Rule to yourselves. There's no science to it. *No tiene ciencia.* Let my Chalupa Rule and Tía Elia guide your hands.

She was always more than happy to guide us, step-by-step, to turn our dreams into reality.

No Tiene Ciencia

There Is No Science to It

CHALUPA RULE TEN

10

EL GORRITO
The Little Hat

With Shouts and Waving of the Hat

A Puros Gritos y Sombrerazos

Prontito:

Sometimes you have to dig deep and find a supply of energy you didn't know you had. It's there waiting for you. This spirit that will take you to the finish line requires you to become your own best cheerleader. Shout encouragement to yourself. Spur yourself on. Sometimes it makes the difference between finishing first and being an also-ran.

A Lo Largo

¡Llegamos a puros gritos y sombrerazos! "Whew, we barely made it!"

The gas tank in the car is way beyond empty. We are running on fumes. There are eight people in the car, all of them biting their nails wondering if we will make it home this time. It's happened many times before. My parents pulled together just enough money to fill the tank for the trip to our intended destination and back. There was no sight-seeing, no taking the scenic route.

Oh, the times we pulled up to the gas station and asked for "Two dollars, regular." Sometimes it was even a "dollar-fifty regular, please."

Each time, we ignored the raised eyebrows from the gas station attendants as they wet our car's whistle. Granted, when I was a child gas was a lot less expensive than it is now but still our fuel purchases ran toward leaving the car *con mucha sed.* Always on the brink of dying of thirst, our ancient, beat-up cars were almost miraculous in their ability to sail up to our house, slightly tipsy from the anemic fumes that remained in their tanks. And, as he heaved a sigh of relief and turned off the engine, our father would always say, *Híjole. Llegamos a puros gritos y sombrerazos.*

Every single time we asked him where that *dicho* came from, and each time, he told us it came from the time of the Mexican cowboys.

My father said that when the cowboys were at the end of a long, exhausting cattle roundup, they always rallied, using shouts and waves of their hats to bring in the herd. Their *gritos* (shouts) and *sombrerazos* (wavings of the hat) provided them with another burst of energy to finish their job.

So, when our old cars were on the verge of running out of gas my father invoked this phrase, apparently envisioning our secondhand car as stubborn cattle that he urged on with shouts and encouragement.

Sometimes in life, when we are trying our hardest, when we are at our most exhausted, all we have left is to shout encouragements to ourselves. All we have to spur us on to the finish line is an enthusiastic "waving of that cowboy hat" over our heads.

That mental picture has helped me many times and that's why it has become one of my favorite Chalupa Rules. It has seen me through some very tough times.

I graduated from college *a puros gritos y sombrerazos.*

Struggling with two jobs and a family to help support, college was an enormous day-to-day struggle. From collecting cans on the side of the road for gas money to missing out on all campus social life, I was surrounded on all sides by tremendous pressures.

I had twitches, one in each eye, to prove it. But still, with internal shouts and waving of the hat, my family and I pressed on to the finish line.

My typewriter, however, almost didn't make it. This vital piece of college equipment spent quite a bit of time in pawn shops. It became a family ritual. Take the typewriter out of hock, write the term papers, and then hock it all over again. Those twenty-five and sometimes forty dollars meant the difference between something to eat and an empty refrigerator so, in the typewriter went. More than once.

And then, after four years of hard work, scholarships, grants, and loans I barely got my diploma.

Not because the two jobs hurt my studies.

Not because of the lack of food and money in the house.

I almost didn't get my diploma because I couldn't afford the twenty-five-dollar graduation fee. Actually, I did have the money, the first time. When graduation time arrived and my family learned of the fee, we pooled our resources. I went to the university's business office, paid the fee, got the receipt, and went home.

My family and I, excited about the upcoming graduation,

never gave it another thought until I was notified by the school that I still owed the fee. Receipt in hand, I returned to the office to prove my case.

A mistake had been made. My "graduation fee" had been credited to my student loan account, as I recall. I was told there was no way to get the money back. I would have to pay the fee again. Twenty-five dollars.

They might as well have asked me for twenty-five million dollars.

My family and I did not have even five dollars to spare. If it wasn't paid, I was not going to be allowed to attend the graduation ceremony. After several phone calls to family members, we learned no one else had that kind of money either.

There was no choice. I had to ask for help. I went to a representative of the business office and asked for a twenty-five dollar loan. I was told, "That would be like robbing Peter to pay Paul." After four years of hard work and having caused no problems at the school, my request was denied.

It was time for this Chalupa Rule to see me through. All we had left was *puros gritos y sombrerazos*. After hours of study, writing papers, and final exams, I used my last ounce of energy, the little that I had left, to make a last-minute round of phone calls.

Fifty-cents. A dollar here. Two dollars there. Thankfully, my relatives contributed what little money they had. Loose change. Twenty-five cents. Slowly but surely, it added up to twenty-five dollars. I had the fee. I walked across that stage and received my diploma.

Now you get the picture of what *gritos y sombrerazos* is all about. When all the chips are down and when the odds are against you, roll up your sleeves and give yourself those "waves of the hat" and "shouts of encouragement" as you do what you need to do to accomplish something in your life. When you don't have the resources to finish a job you can get by on pure enthusiasm, energy, and hope.

By conducting an inner dialogue with ourselves we can call upon hidden reserves of energy and spirit. Like the old Mexican cowboys who, with whistles, waves, and shouts would make it through the last miles of a grueling cattle drive, we can also shout encouragement to ourselves. We can raise the volume of that inner voice to make it our own "cheerleader" urging us on to the finish line. *A puros gritos y sombrerazos/*With pure shouts and waves we can spur ourselves on to success.

You may not have *dinero* but you do have the power to encourage yourself.

You may not have a stack of credit cards, but you do have the power to charge up your determination.

You may not have stocks and bonds, but you do have people around you who, twenty-five cents at a time, invest in your future.

A puros gritos y sombrerazos. Sometimes all you have *left* to go on is pure energy. Your "fuel tank" may be empty of material possessions, but your spiritual fuel tank can always be full.

You may have an empty bank account but faith in yourself and your family will never run out. It's your choice to call upon those endless reserves.

Twenty-five dollars almost got in the way of my getting that diploma. But this Chalupa Rule made sure it was safely in my hands that graduation day in 1978, making me the first family member to graduate from college.

Shouts and waves of the hat? To encourage myself? No problem. I can shout loud. I can wave my hat of determination in broad, wide circles so that everyone can see that a Spanish proverb from our rich and beautiful culture can see me through.

It can see you through as well.

When I use the word *gringo* I mean it with a lot of love and respect. It's just our Tex-Mex word for Anglo-Americans. Well, this Chalupa Rule is well-served by two very brilliant *gringos* whose words I want to share with you right now.

In their day, Noel Coward and President Calvin Coolidge must have done some serious *gritos y sombrerazos* in order to come up with the following words.

They are so important to me that I cut them out and pasted them on my wall at home so that when I need some "shouts and waving of the hat" to push me to the finish line, they are always there.

President Coolidge, *bienvenido* to the world of the Chalupa Rules:

> *Nothing in the world can take the place of persistence. Talent will not; nothing is more common than successful people with talent. Genius will not; unrewarded genius is almost a proverb. Education will not; the world is full of educated derelicts. Persistence and determination alone are omnipotent. The slogan, "Press On" has solved and always will solve the problems of the human race.*
>
> —Calvin Coolidge

Mr. Coward, if you will:

> *Thousands of people have talent. I might as well congratulate you for having eyes in your head. The one and only thing that counts is: Do you have staying power?*
>
> —Noel Coward

A Puros Gritos y Sombrerazos

With Shouts and Waving of the Hat You Can Reach Your Goal

CHALUPA RULE ELEVEN

11

EL CAZO
The Container

You Can Never Save Time.
You Can Only Spend It

El Tiempo No Se Ahorra. Solamente Se Puede Gastar

Prontito:

Trying to "save time" is a losing battle. It's more important to invest energy into the time you "spend." When you concentrate on time as an element to be "used up," you place more emphasis on quantity than quality of seconds, minutes, and hours.

A Lo Largo

Every now and then, when you are playing a round of Mexican bingo, the image of *el cazo* will pop up. Some dictionaries describe it as a "ladle" or "dipper" but the way it is depicted in the game, it looks more like a large, empty brass pan. This makes it perfect as the image for this Chalupa Rule.

We spend days of worry and nights without sleep *preocupados*, fretting about how to save time. If you try to fill up some imaginary container with time that you have saved, you will never succeed. That is because time can never be saved, it can only be spent.

Stick your hand in Niagara Falls just before the water goes over the edge and try to stop it from flowing. You will have the same success when you try to dip your hand into time and try to stop it from moving forward. You cannot fill your empty pockets or your *bolsillo*, your handbag, with minutes, hours, and seconds.

Working in television news, you quickly learn that every second counts. A newscast is filled with the news of the day, breaking news that comes in at the last moment, interesting features, weather, and sports. Every moment is filled, every available second is used. All of the time is "spent and not saved," *el tiempo no es ahorrado, es gastado.* You cannot "save" the time from one program and invest it into the show that comes after it. The time allotted is used to its fullest, from start to finish.

Some interesting things happen when you reverse the concept and stop trying to save up time and instead focus on how you will "spend" it. First, you concentrate more on the quality of the moment, instead of turning it into numbers in an "accounting book" in your head, juggling seconds, minutes, and hours and trying to come up with a balanced "checkbook" of time saved.

"Spend" your time focusing on the job at hand and paying attention to detail instead of thinking how you can shave a few minutes off the task.

"Spend" your time with your children reading a book together from start to finish without worrying if *la lavada*, the laundry, is done.

When you spend your time instead of save it, eventually you will realize there is more time for everything. Somehow, time becomes *una amiga* instead of an enemy.

When you say, "I saved thirty minutes of time by taking a shortcut to work," I challenge you to take me to this wonderful bank where you have your time saved up in a special account, ready to be spent later. I don't think so. Instead, show me how you spent the time you "saved." To me, that is the more important issue.

Okay, *felicidades*, you saved *una media hora. ¿Cómo gastaste el tiempo?* How did you spend that time? It has to be used up somehow.

Time, as a concept, doesn't know it has been saved. It just keeps moving forward, oblivious to our efforts to save it. As my older *tíos* used to say in their playful mix of English and Spanish, "It no make-eh no le hace." It doesn't matter to time that you are desperately trying to save it.

It doesn't need saving. It needs spending.

Your *Cazo*/Container will never fill up with "time." Instead, pour time onto your family, your friends, and your projects. Cutting corners is not always a good thing.

Give time to your endeavors; lavish them with wave upon wave of time, creating a better final result.

El Tiempo No Se Ahorra. Solamente Se Puede Gastar

You Can Never Save Time. You Can Only Spend It

CHALUPA RULE TWELVE

EL MUNDO
Atlas

The More You Put It Off, the More You Put It On

Mientras Más Lo Pospones, Más Te Pesará

Prontito:

Delaying a job or a chore only makes it heavier, weighing you down. It's like adding pound after pound on your shoulders until you feel you are carrying the entire planet around in the form of unfinished business and tasks left undone. Each time you finish a job or project, you lighten your load and make room for new things to happen in your life. Clean house.

Lighten your load. Take the weight of the world off your shoulders.

A Lo Largo

The well-muscled Atlas, holding up the entire planet, is trying his best to bear the incredible weight. Every fiber of his being is stressing out, fighting to keep the heavy load overhead.

He is wrestling with the weight, *le está haciendo la lucha*. It makes you wonder just how long he'll be able to hold the world up over his head.

That muscleman represents each and every one of us. The ever-increasing weight he bears represents all the things we put off in life. Every chore we avoid, every phone call we don't return, every pile of laundry that adds up.

We all do it. Procrastinate, that is. In my family, we call it being *decidioso*, undecided about doing something. Dust gathers on the furniture, the bills pile up, and the homework becomes this giant monster that grows so big and scary we are afraid to touch it. So, it all goes undone until it's a mountain of procrastination.

This Chalupa Rule boils the problem of procrastination down to this one, simple but powerful truth:

The more you put it off, the more you put it on.

When you postpone something you need to do, it weighs more and more on you until you feel you are carrying the weight of the entire world on your shoulders. When you finally perform the task you are putting off, a great weight is lifted. So don't put it off; you only put it on more.

Look in your closet, your garage, and even in your bedroom. There are monsters lurking everywhere. They are so scary that we've decided to put them out of our mind, making them invisible so that they don't bother us.

Those monsters are boxes and boxes of "stuff," *cosas*. All of the papers, photos, and other documents that are not on the main stage of daily life are shoved into those boxes and cabinets and drawers. Out of sight out of mind, right?

Creo que no. I don't think so.

Those unfinished chores use up a little bit of our energy every day. It's like leaving the refrigerator door open just a little, all day. That poor fridge goes into overload, trying to cool the entire space, all because the door is open, wasting energy.

Me confieso. I confess. I wrestle with this Chalupa Rule everyday. The temptation is always there to put something off, to avoid it until a *mañana* that never comes. Like the open refrigerator door, that unfinished business uses up some brain *jugo* every day. Brain juice we could put to better use.

The more you put it off, the more you put it on. I was this rule's biggest offender, but at least in one case I fought the monster boxes and won.

Many of my "important papers" were *still in boxes* after three, maybe four, moves. I *thought* they were important. Frankly, I couldn't even remember what this Chicano chipmunk had stored away. The boxes, from move to move, mocked me with their now mysterious identification labels, "Miscellaneous," "Important Papers," or simply "Items."

Had my life collapsed into an anonymous pile of yellowing papers and crumpled-up bills from department stores that had closed years ago?

These boxes, heavy and filled with mystery had cost me:

- Money (For shipping every single time that I moved)

- Chiropractic sessions (For every time I got a sore back from moving them myself)

- Embarrassment (You see, some of the offending, hibernating boxes had planted themselves in my home office. I thought that I had cleverly disguised their presence by draping crisp, white bedsheets over their rude, bulky shapes. All I had succeeded in doing was to transform them into snow-white cubes of wasted space. They sat in lazy indifference, a pile of giant marshmallows)

To get an idea of exactly how much this lingering mess weighs down on your *mundo*, do this exercise. Just don't throw out your back.

Have a friend help you. Pick up one of the boxes of your accumulated "stuff" and place it on your shoulder. Let it weigh down on you. Feel the weight? Are you all of a sudden feeling extra *gordito*, fatter, with that dead weight pushing down on your body? It should come as no surprise. That dead weight slows your life down. Now multiply that box by all the boxes you have hanging around your house, your apartment, your office, or your building. Imagine all of them stacked up, one on top of the other and placed on your shoulders like the entire planet the Mexican muscleman of this Chalupa Rule carries on his back.

Ouch. If that is not enough to get you going, then read on. Something happened to kick-start this Chalupa Rule. I found an article in the *New York Times* that included the following quote: "Life is a daily battle against the accretion of tiny entropies." There, in an article by David Rakoff, was the explanation for all the little *cositas* that cluttered my life and distracted me from work and play.

Pero primero, vamos a traduzir esta teoría tan complicada. Let's translate this complicated theory.

First: We all know that life is a daily battle. Second: What the heck are accretions and entropies? Here we go. Accretion means that something grows by layers, little-by-little, one on top of the other. Entropy means "a measure of disorder that exists in a system." Translated into English that we all can understand, "Life is a daily battle against the accretion of tiny entropies" means that we are in a constant fight against disorder and mess that keep layering themselves on our lives.

That dust that, every day, falls on your furniture is not going to magically go away; it is going to make a daily attack, layering itself into a mess. At first it may not be that visible but I guarantee you it is definitely growing. That can only mean

that we have to get used to the idea that our fight against disorder is a daily one, one that is not going to go away.

To quote millions of mariachis, *Ay, ay, ay*. Now, what to do
about it? Well, the only way to relieve the weight is to take it
off. That is the only way, *mi amigo*.

I admit to you that some of those boxes were ten years old.
I have nieces and nephews younger than that. Shame on me.

I was intimidated, almost as if some living creature, perhaps the legendary *Chupacabras* or *La Llorona* of Latino folklore, had roused itself from deep sleep and roared in my face.
It sent me screaming down the streets of Manhattan, a crazy
Mexican running away in terror from his storage boxes. *Qúe
bonito*.

I pulled back the cracked, ancient, and yellowing packing
tape and opened first one cardboard flap and then the other.

Ay, Díos mío. There *were* monsters inside. Monsters of mess.
Demons of dust. Skeletons of paper. *This* is what I have been
carrying with me all of these years? *Qúe verguenza*. Too bad I
am brown-skinned and so couldn't blush. I was ashamed of
myself. Pounds and pounds, *libras sobre libras* of *mugrego*/junk.

Granted, there were some valuable items mixed with the
mess, family photos, car titles, insurance documents, and
Social Security information. But, other than that, *nada mucho*.
I even discovered empty, useless envelopes. I found old
notepads with only one or two pages that had been used and
dried up pens and broken pencils. It was time to stop the "accretion of tiny entropies." And there was no putting off the in-
evitable; I planned to lift the tremendous weight off my
shoulders, today. Okay, well, tomorrow or maybe the day after
that. I didn't say that I was perfect. These Chalupa Rules are a
daily struggle for me as well.

However, one day I had nothing else to do but stare at the
enemy. Suddenly, I thought I noticed the boxes smirking at
me from under their sheets. I know they did it on purpose,
twisting their fading permanent marker mouths into the

smile of a challenge. Time to take action. It was me versus *las maldito cajas de carton*. Those darn cardboard boxes would mock me no more.

Thank goodness my family had taken me to the Friday night wrestling matches on the west side of San Antonio. These boxes were my wrestling opponents. I was *Mario el Macho* (insert big laugh here) versus the *Mil Mascaras* of the cardboard box world. The match was on. Paper-after-paper, empty-envelope-after-empty-envelope, the cardboard boxes gave up their contents to the mighty muscle of this Chalupa Rule. I filled three large trash bags with *mugrego* and only a small pile of important papers remained.

Here is some great advice for cleaning out your mess, if you have one. This comes from Ron Alford, owner of Disastermasters, a New York City cleaning company.

Disastermasters specializes in clearing out houses and apartments of people who are at the most extreme end of the clutter scale. I am talking about apartments where the trash is piled up three feet high or more in every room. If you want to see for yourself go to www.disastermasters.com.

Ron says when you are cleaning out your house, use this valuable rule. Pick something up. Hold it in your hands. If in thirty seconds you can't decide whether to keep it or throw it away, throw it away.

I wish you had been there when I finally reached the bottom of those *cajas*. I could almost hear them whimpering and yelping as they ran away, licking their wounds in defeat. Take that. *Mario el Macho* won the first round. Frankly, it took several rounds of carton wrestling before I emptied the arena of opponents.

Boy, it feels good, or as we Tejanos say, *de aquella*, when there is only clean, empty space where ugly, mocking boxes had been before. Guess what? That weight that pressed down on my shoulders went away. "Poof."

I felt like I had gone on a diet. And I guess I had.

Mientra Más Lo Pospones, Más Te Pesará

The More You Put It Off, the More You Put It On

CHALUPA RULE THIRTEEN

13

LA CAMPANA
The Bell

You Are Always Going to Be a Student

Siempre Serás Estudiante

Prontito:

The desire to learn new things and explore new ideas should continue beyond graduation. School is in session for the rest of your life. The minute you stop learning or wanting to learn, you become a "dinosaur," in danger of becoming extinct while others move forward, learning new techniques and innovations.

Keep your love of learning alive and share it with younger people. Select a library book from a new section you've never entered before. Learn something just for the fun of it. Take guitar lessons. Do crossword puzzles. Teach yourself a new song. Don't worry about what others think. Learn for the joy of learning. Even if you play the guitar badly or can't sing a note, IT'S OKAY. Perform for an audience of one: you.

A Lo Largo

Years ago, when I was still getting my feet wet in the business of broadcast journalism, station management brought in consultants. What is a consultant? Well, imagine someone walking into your office or classroom and videotaping your every word and movement. Then, they sit down with you and review your work, dissecting everything you do. They analyze everything, from the way you write the news, to the way you deliver it, and even the way you look.

At first, it is an eerie feeling to have a complete stranger peer into the depths of your professional soul. It's like you're taken aboard an alien spacecraft where superior beings perform their experiments on you. These consultants might as well wear lab coats. They proceed to take you apart, bit by bit, giving you in-depth suggestions and harsh, unvarnished criticism about who you are as a journalist and as a broadcast communicator. I have heard every type of comment that can be made, both constructive and downright silly. However, I have learned important techniques when it comes to writing television news and to delivering it properly. Consultants have also made very useful suggestions about vocal delivery and physical presence.

Among the more creative suggestions: "Drink ginseng tea before you go on the air." I am still trying to figure that one out.

Then there is this advice, "Put the pencil down while you anchor the news." I guess holding a pencil in my hand while I'm on the air gets in the way of viewers' abilities to absorb the news of the day.

But, despite the occasional doses of unusual advice and bizarre pointers, I also learned important tools that help me when I go on the air to deliver the news. I took notes diligently and put the consultant's advice into practice, tracking my progress. If I wasn't chosen for a session, I was always the first in line, volunteering for one. With every tip, every bit of advice, I felt my work improved.

For me, class is always in session. I always look forward to learning something new. Do You?

I always put this Chalupa Rule into practice. It is one that I handcrafted to help me always remember this fact of life: You are always going to be a student, even if you graduate high school or college. Even if you finish a vocational or business school, it doesn't matter.

You are always going to be a student.

Your ears should always be perked up and alert, waiting to hear that *campana*, that school bell ringing in the distance.

But there are people who are insulted when they are offered advice, whether it comes in the form of official coaching or perhaps some tips from a coworker. Some people feel like they are finished products. They are convinced they have rolled off the "assembly line of life" as a complete package, a turn-key operation that only needs to be let loose into the professional world so that they can release their dazzling fireworks of talent.

Look out world, here I come!

But if you stop being a student of life, all movement forward, all progress, stops.

Look out world, I'm extinct!

A long time ago, I worked with people who were insulted at having to work with a consultant. I got the impression that they thought they were finished products, that there wasn't a single new thing that they needed to learn. Despite the free speech coaching, the pointers about improving performance, and the advice on how to better communicate with the viewer, they resisted going through the consultation process. That confused me. If there is even the smallest possibility of learning something new, leap at the chance.

If, at work, you are offered the opportunity to attend a seminar, it should be as if a school bell starts ringing in your head. Head to class with a hunger for learning. You can even call it a personal process of evolution. Learning new ways to do things makes you more adaptable to changes in the work environment.

Many species in the plant and animal world are extinct because they became too specialized. When the environment changed, they did not catch up fast enough and their kind *se desapareció*. Poof. Gone.

The same goes for people. It's okay to be specialized in your work and your interests but beware. If the work or technological environment changes you could go the way of the Dodo bird. While you work in your field of expertise, you should also cultivate other interests that are related to your field, *por si a caso*. Just in case. If you are resistant to coaching, to advice and counseling, then you become a dinosaur.

If you don't keep up with the changes in the workplace, then it's "Hasta la vista, baby."

Sometimes people at work think, "Just wait until I get that big promotion. Then I'll show them what I can really do." On the job, from day one, we should perform as if we already have that big promotion, so that those in charge can see what we can do right away.

It doesn't take a lot of money to be a student for life. Not if you know where to look. My interest in theater crashed head-on with a big problem. I didn't have any money for acting, singing, or dancing classes. That's where community theater steps in to fill the financial blanks. I auditioned for a production and even though I only got a very small part, I enjoyed free voice lessons, dance classes, and acting advice. All it cost me was time. I didn't have money to spend but I did have time to invest.

You rarely see a good student without a pen and notebook handy. So if you are going to be a student for life then you should do the same thing. A small, inexpensive notebook stuck in your back pocket will do just fine. Any cheap pen or pencil in the front pocket will serve the purpose. Before I could afford a portable computer, that little notebook was my "Latino laptop." It never ran out of batteries, never crashed, and if I didn't fall in a mud puddle, never erased my ideas.

As we try to get a handle on how to use this Chalupa Rule we should keep in mind another type of student in the United

States. They are the Latinos who had to abandon their educations in order to raise a family.

At one time, it seemed as if giving up your education was a one-way street. Putting aside the classroom usually meant an irreversible death sentence for dreams of furthering an education. I have to look no farther than my own family for proof the process can be reversed. My mother dropped out of high school in the eleventh grade. The rest of her life included marriage, domestic abuse, poverty, and eventually divorce, but not the completion of her education. While I attended college and my sisters pursued their educations, my mother decided to do something about her lack of a diploma.

Those afternoon homework sessions are some of my fondest memories. I worked on my college degree, my sisters finished their homework, and our mother sat there at the dinner table with us, concentrating with all her might on getting her G.E.D. Finally, at the end of her night classes, my mother held her life's dream in her hands: her General Equivalency Diploma. They held a special ceremony and, as proud and excited as I have ever seen her, my mother walked across the graduation stage to accept her reward. She was the living example of this Chalupa Rule, that you can and should be a student at every stage of your life.

Un estudiante para siempre. A student, forever.

If there is a family member or friend in your life who dreams of finishing their high school education, then use the insights of this rule and also of Chalupa Rule Number Four, be their Diana Rodríguez and help them reach their goal. To find out about Diana Rodríguez, see Chalupa Rule 20.

When you think of a new generation, people of the same age come to mind. I envision a different sort of "new generation" of Latinos. They include an eighty-year-old Latina taking a night class for fun, a thirty-year-old Latino studying quantum physics as a hobby, and a thirteen-year-old Latina learning the intricacies of economics. The new generation includes Latinos of all ages and backgrounds, *unidos en la edu-cacion,* united in education.

Avanzando juntos. Advancing together.

Part of that advancement has to include reading. If you do not read for pleasure, for the sheer enjoyment of it, don't expect your children to do the same. Open a book in front of them. Force yourself to read even just a few paragraphs.

Do you have books all over the house? In the living room? In their bedroom? In the kitchen? This does not have to be an expense at all. Your local library has enough books to last all of you for a lifetime.

Open the floodgates of reading by encouraging your children to read just about everything. Comic books. Short stories. Let your imagination run wild. But you should be students together, wandering the library stacks, deciding which of the books and authors are your favorites.

As a child, I had a passion for reading and I'd read all the available books in the house. Only trips to the library satisfied my need for new books, new ideas.

There was one other resource but it was limited. Occasionally, local grocery stores offered sets of encyclopedias at very low prices. For example, volume "A" and volume "B" cost twenty-nine cents a piece. Those we quickly snapped up, excited at the prospect of finally having a complete set of encyclopedias at home. Then the promotion ended and from that point on all of the volumes were more expensive. Volumes "C" through "Z" jumped in price, sometimes to as high as $1.29 a piece. $1.29! *Olvídate.* No way that our limited budget allowed for that extravagance. So, there on our one little bookshelf sat several brands of encyclopedias, *World Book* and others, A through B only.

I joked that I could never be asked any questions on subjects that ran from C through Z, I could only be asked A through B questions.

Mexicans from A through B.

If my family had relied only on those lonely A-B encyclopedia collections, our knowledge would have been just as limited. But if you are resourceful and keep your eyes and ears open to the opportunity of learning, the world will open up for you.

We wanted to buy books. We wanted to subscribe to magazines, but as with so many other Latino families, the money wasn't there.

According to recent trends however, it seems that Latinos now have greater buying power. Does that translate into the purchase of books and other reading material that can help us "always be a student"? As I mentioned before, these Chalupa Rules don't waste your time. So, here are some pretty disappointing statistics. In his book, *The New Mainstream,* author Guy García points out the differences in buying habits between African Americans and Latinos:

> *A Consumer Expenditure Survey conducted in 2003 by the U.S. Department of Commerce shows that Hispanics and African Americans differ considerably in how they spend across a number of consumer categories. For example, African Americans significantly outspend Hispanics on books, contributions, education, health care, household furnishings, housing insurance, and media while Hispanics spend more on alcoholic beverages, consumer electronics, housewares, sports, and toys.*

¿Qué nos pasa? What is happening to us? Clearly, the *centavitos* we now have need some redistribution in the budget department. And according to Mr. García, there are definitely more of those pennies to spread around:

> *. . . the data indicates ethnic consumer spending will continue to increase into the foreseeable future. U.S. Hispanic population growth rates and purchasing power are both rising faster than the general population.*

Hmm. Our purchasing power is going up but our purchase of *libros* can't keep up with the alcohol and stereos and toys we throw into our shopping carts? It seems that living up to the true spirit of this Chalupa Rule is a big challenge for all of us. Now that we know the numbers there is plenty that we can do about it.

Many families are extremely busy, working all day and then struggling to get food on the table. Time can be your enemy, making it hard to go out and shop for books. But even that problem can be overcome. All you have to do is open the daily newspaper. Free community classes and seminars are offered all the time.

For the price of a daily paper you and your family can explore a bilingual supplement that runs stories in Spanish and English, side by side. An example of that is *Conexión,* a supplement that's included in the *San Antonio Express-News.* There are hundreds like them around the country.

They are all ways that you can live up to this Chalupa Rule.

Then, instead of Latinos from A-to-B, it will be "Latinos from A-to-Infinity."

The sound of opportunity, of new lessons to be learned, comes in the form of a *campana.*

Look forward to the sound of the ringing bell.

Siempre Serás Estudiante

**You Are Always Going
to Be a Student**

LA CALAVERA
The Skull

One "No" Is Not Going to Kill You

Un "No" No Te Mata

Prontito:

Are you deathly afraid of the word "no"? Does it feel like you die just a little every time someone turns down your requests? You have to dare yourself to ask questions. Take the risk and you will be surprised that most of the time there is a "yes" where you think a "no" might be lurking instead. "No" is just a word. It isn't going to kill you.

A Lo Largo

This Chalupa Rule is all about *miedo*/fear. The image is *La Calavera* from the traditional game of Mexican bingo. The chilling skull and crossbones are designed to scare you, to make you run for cover.

For example, you ask a question and someone says "no."

"Boo!"

Run for your life!

When we ask a question of someone, whether it's to ask for a raise, for permission, or even just for a small favor, we all dread hearing the word "no."

It's like a little death every time we hear the word "no." It feels like the end of the world. Stare that "no" in the face and lose your fear of it. Like the chalupa image, it is only an illusion.

There are many times when I have asked a question and have been told "no." A request for an interview is turned down after numerous phone calls and pleas. A job application and an interview turns into "No, we are not going to hire you." A request for a discount on a purchase becomes, "No, we don't give discounts." Despite all those "No's," I am still here. *Dios mío*, this Chalupa Rule is right. *Un "no" no te mata.* One "no" is not going to kill you.

I put this into practice every day. Practice. Practice. Practice.

Many times I find myself thinking, "Just imagine what would have happened if I didn't ask certain questions?"

My mother found the strength to ask about the possibility of the family buying a brand-new home. We applied to an FHA 235 housing program. With two hundred dollars down (money that we had to scrape together) we had our new house. Despite some family opposition and negative thinking on the part of some relatives, she pushed ahead. With her forward thinking and her bravery in asking questions that never would have been asked before, we moved into our new home.

For many years we had lived in three rooms and had no hot water. Eight people were cramped into those tight quarters. The possibility of having a new house seemed as remote a dream as me one day setting foot on a planet in an entirely different universe. My mother made the phone calls. She got the ball rolling. And before we knew it we had hot water, an actual hallway, and three bedrooms. We actually got to watch the house being built. This was an incredible experience and an amazing achievement for our family. And it all happened because she dared to ask the questions that everyone else was afraid to ask: "We have no credit, no bank account, and very little income, but can we still apply for an FHA 235 government home?"

The self-esteem and confidence that the move to a new home gave our family is immeasurable. We never dreamed that it could be possible. It was possible because of bravery.

More questions that you have to dare yourself to ask:

What kinds of scholarships are available?
Do you have a grace period?
Can you wait one more week for the payment?
What if I pay you half now and promise (in writing) that
    I will pay the rest in two weeks' time?

In my life, I have asked all of those questions out of sheer desperation and necessity. If you explain yourself clearly and with total honesty, you will be surprised at how helpful and cooperative people can be in your time of need.

After I adopted my dog, Huitzi, from the Humane Society of New York, I discovered through testing that he had cancer, lymphoma to be exact. The treatments are extremely time-consuming and expensive. The time element I could handle, but the money was another story. This was a terrible time for my family. My mother was in the last stages of scleroderma, a devastating disease that crippled her body and also meant up to a thousand dollars a month in medication. That, plus all the financial responsibilities of supporting a family, strained my finances to the limit. Chemotherapy for Huitzi was necessary. It was also a financial burden that I wasn't sure I could handle.

That is where this Chalupa Rule comes into the picture.

After a deep, heartfelt conversation with Sandra De Feo from the Humane Society, the problem was resolved. I explained my situation and asked for help. There is no shame in asking for help when you need it. It was also my only option.

Thanks to their wonderful, deep caring for abandoned animals like Huitzi, they understood the heartache and pressures of caring for an ailing, aging dog. The chemotherapy began and Huitzi's life was saved.

I asked for help and they did not say "no."

The fear of the word "no," if conquered, can open up many doors.

In negotiating a television contract, any agent will tell you that a request for a high starting salary is always greeted with a resounding "no." Agents never take the first "no," they work through it until a middle ground is reached. You should never take the first "no" either.

The most vivid memory I have of being afraid to ask a question goes back to my high school years. It was Christmas and there was very little money for presents, let alone a Christmas tree. My family and I pulled together what little extra money we had and went to the local nursery. It was one day before Christmas and just about all the trees were gone. The only ones left were ready for the trash bin. Our hope of getting a Christmas tree for my little sisters was gone. We had twenty dollars we had naïvely hoped would cover the price of a tree, lights, decorations, and tinsel. I don't know what made us think that was possible.

We all stood there, my father, my mother, my sisters, and I, staring at their centerpiece display. It was a white Christmas tree, dripping with lights, tinsel, and an array of twinkling, exquisite holiday decorations. This Christmas fantasy was the most beautiful tree we had ever seen. I don't know what came over me. Perhaps it was born of desperation, of a hope that anything is possible. Perhaps it was the desire to put a smile on my family's face. In reality, I think I asked the question because there was no option left other than to go home. "How much is that tree?" I heard myself asking the Christmas tree salesman. My family looked at me in surprise and astonishment, as if I had gone out of my mind.

"How much do you have?" the salesman responded. I asked him to please repeat the question.

"Twenty dollars," I said, feeling in my pants pocket the wad of ones and fives that made up the bulk of our holiday budget.

"Take it," he said, explaining that they hadn't been able to sell it and wanted to get rid of it.

I will never forget how I felt as they wrapped up our tree and we triumphantly carried it home.

The tree lit up our home, but most important of all it lit up my sisters' faces. I would not trade that memory for anything.

And it all happened because I dared to ask a question. Now, I ask away, knowing that one single, solitary "no" is not the terrifying monster I had imagined it to be.

Un "No" No Te Mata

One "No" Is Not Going to Kill You

CHALUPA RULE FIFTEEN

15

LA BOTA
The Boot

Give It Shine!

¡Dale Chine!

Prontito:

Every job you do, every task you perform should shine. Polish up your performance with that extra dose of concentration and detail. You can also add brilliance and gloss to your self-esteem by knowing you've gone the extra mile for a "job well done."

A Lo Largo

I was moments away from my first anchoring experience in New York City. My palms dripped with perspiration, my voice trembled, and I wondered what I was doing there in the first place. So much rode on my performance. The family I supported was at the top of that list. *Mi familia* was at home in Texas, anxiously awaiting my phone call to tell them how it all went. They were proud and excited. I was about to pass out from *nervios*.

Then, just before the light on the camera turned red, indicating the show was on, a phrase came back to me from the streets of San Antonio. It echoed loud and clear in the enormous television studio. Although no one heard it but me, it was as reassuring as a friendly pat on the back from a good *amigo*. The words calmed me and made me feel at home. The words were:

¡Dale chine!

"Give it shine! Give it all you've got! Go for it!"

I gave it my best. I anchored the show. I didn't pass out.

Pronounced "dá-leh chine" (the word "shine" pronounced Tex-Mex style with a hard "ch"), this Chalupa Rule helped me through that experience. I took a deep breath and even though the nerves were still there, the words from my culture, my home base, gave me the spirit to do the job.

This phrase comes to you directly from the streets, from the *barrios*, from the mouths of the *Pachucos*.

¡Dale chine!

Pachucos existed on the sidelines of Mexican American society. They were fading into history when I was growing up. Their time to shine had been in the forties and fifties.

It seemed to me that just about every family had a *primo* or *tío* who either belonged to some sort of Mexican gang or simply copied their style and way of dress. Look through old family photo albums, leaf through the pages, and you will find their images glaring back at you.

Their hair dripped with Three Flowers Brilliantine. They dressed in baggy pants, usually khaki, and accessorized them with three-quarter length sleeves, orange "roach killer" shoes, and wide-brimmed hats on their heads.

Pachucos had their own way of talking. It was a spicy, mysterious combination of Spanish, English, and words that seemed to have been conjured up from discrimination, street violence, and the anxieties of teenage boys growing up wedged between the Mexican and Anglo cultures.

Out of this boiling pot of *Mexicanismo*, they strutted into the *barrios*, their fedoras tilted over one eye creating the illusion of a permanent, sexy wink for any young woman who walked by them. Their uniforms of baggy khaki pants and tattooed forearms told the world that they belonged to the realm of the *Pachuco*.

By the time I was in junior high, *Pachucos* were already strutting their way into the Mexican sunset, but there were still enough of them around to threaten to beat us all up after school or linger on the sidelines of school dances, hoping to snag a *rucita*, a chick, for a grinding, *Pachuco*-style slow dance.

When *Pachucos* spoke, out of their mouths came an astonishing torrent of words that very often only they could understand.

Órale vato translates roughly, in my opinion, to "Hey, dude." I could go on and on until I have you totally immersed in the sound and flavor of the *Pachuco*. However, there is only one phrase that I want to share with you.

Whenever *Pachuco*-type guys danced, drove down the street honking their low-rider horns really loud, or simply lived the fast *barrio*-life, one phrase always stood out.

That phrase was *¡Dale chine!*

"Give it shine!" "Go for it!" or "Give it all you've got!"

Think of polishing a pair of shoes the old-fashioned way, buffing with a heavy brush dripping with thick, black polish. The harder you buffed, the shinier the shoes became.

Well, I imagined *Pachucos* borrowed that phrase and transported it into their world. Because of their Tex-Mex accents the word "shine" transformed into the word *"chine"* and *dale* is a Tejano way of saying give it. Get it?

Whether at school, at work, or at home, this Chalupa Rule tells us to "Give it shine!" Tackle all of your responsibilities with gusto. Whatever you do, make sure it has the best polish or shine that you can possibly give it.

The *Pachucos* gave the rest of us Latinos this phrase. We can use it to live our lives in the United States with the bravado and spirit of our brown brothers in the baggy pants and roach killer shoes.

Simply think to yourself, *¡Dale chine! ¡Dale chine! ¡Dale chine!*

You can also use this Chalupa Rule to polish up your feelings of self-worth. Years of accepting charity can badly dent and scar your self-esteem. You feel inadequate, as if you are to blame for the family's poverty. We were not alone. Many families around us went through the same thing.

Some even had less than we did. But no matter how low the financial reserves got or how desperate your situation became, there were always paths to giving yourself a boost of encouragement and making the best of a situation.

That's where *¡Dale chine!* steps in to save the day.

If you have to wear someone else's old clothes every day, wear them with pride and confidence as if they were new. Give it shine. It's all in the attitude.

If you have a rusty old car, drive it as if it just rolled off the assembly line.

If you are feeling low and ghosts of abuse from the past come back to haunt you, there are ways to turn on your inner light.

¡Dale chine! just might do the trick.

And there is more.

When you work on a project, this Chalupa Rule will never let you forget that the overall polish and professionalism of your work will be noted and remembered for a long time.

When you perform a task, large or small, this saying can

give you the juice to take yourself beyond the average into the land of ¡*Exelente!*

The shouts of the *Pachuco* and the attention to detail that my father invested into the smallest of chores gave birth to this Chalupa Rule.

When I was a little boy, every now and then I would stop running around the streets on the west side of San Antonio, Texas, long enough to watch my father polish his good pair of shoes.

He worked very hard during the week as a butcher at one or the other of the meat-packing plants. During his early morning, grueling, and very-messy work hours, he had to wear, for his protection, thick, heavy rubber-soled work boots. They protected his feet from the treacherously slippery, wet floors of the workplace. They also provided a cushion of safety between him and the brutally sharp knives that he used in his work.

Every now and then, for special occasions such as a family wedding, he rescued his nice pair of shoes from the closet and took them out for a well-deserved spin on the dance floor. He always dressed up his shoes with the polishing technique he learned while serving in the Army.

I watched in wide-eyed amazement as those scuffed, battered, sleepy shoes woke up under the rhythmic "buff-buff" see-saw he performed, using his trusty polishing brush to dance the bristles across the tops of his only good pair of shoes.

All it took to transform those discount store *zapatos* into a pair of outrageously shiny, walking mirrors was:

1. A little, dented can of cheap polish, scented with the promise of a *baile*, a dance that put his shoes through their happy paces of polkas, cumbias, and sexy cha-cha-chas.

2. A heavy, beat-up shoe brush, its thick, manly spine made of heavily varnished wood. It was studded with

an infinity of bristles made fragrant and baby-soft by countless other expectant afternoons spent coaxing life from a hard-won pair of dancing shoes.

3. And finally, a wide strip of flannel, its surface smeared with black. It was barely recognizable from its previous existence as a work shirt. Given a new job after it was retired, the piece of cloth gave the shoes their final polish before they stepped out to dance.

Those shoes were brilliant. In no way did they resemble the dusty, humble pair of *zapatos* that slept in the closet.

In order to give them their appealing new gloss all that was needed were simple, inexpensive supplies and some enthusiastic swipes of the polishing cloth. It's all in the enthusiasm.

What are some ways to inject *¡Dale chine!* into your life? Well, like my dad's shoe-shining project, you don't have to spend any money at all.

When you finish a project, give it an extra *ojo*. That extra eye you scan over your work will invariably catch a mistake that was invisible before. It is tempting to assume that a project is finished before you are completely satisfied that it's done to the highest standards.

In the business of television news, reporters and photographers shoot a story then go back to the station to begin the editing process. When the report is ready, a manager views the finished piece for final approval. So many times, mistakes are caught, facts are corrected, and shots are rearranged to give the report the solid foundation it needs to be air-worthy.

Your finished products should all be spot-checked for accuracy and polish. There is nothing like an extra pair of eyes that can review your work. Find a coworker you trust, whose opinion you value, and make a "deal" with them. You review their work and they review yours. Not so much for content and material but for simple grammar, punctuation you might have missed, and writing you can improve.

No matter what line of work you are in, you can find ways to polish up the finished product. Reading or checking something once or twice is simply not enough. You have to study your work in depth, take it apart, and put it back together. Dive deep into the heart of your work and see if it really ticks.

Only you can give the final polish to your efforts. By saying *¡Dale chine!*, and really meaning it, your work will be as shiny and wonderfully presentable as my father's shoes when, resplendent in their coat of polish and confidence, they stepped out on the dance floor for a dazzling night of dancing.

¡Dale Chine!

Give It Shine!

CHALUPA RULE SIXTEEN

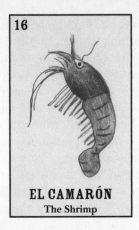

16

EL CAMARÓN
The Shrimp

He Who Falls Asleep Will Be Swept Away by the Current

Camarón Que Se Duerme, Se Lo Lleva la Corriente

Prontito:

Is your life filled with unreturned phone calls and opportunities you ignore? Perhaps you are just floating along in life instead of swimming vigorously toward every wonderful possibility that comes your way. Don't fall asleep in the waters of good fortune and potential. If you do, the current will simply sweep you away.

A Lo Largo

If we were all brave enough to be completely honest with ourselves, we could write an entire book, *un libro muy triste*. This sad book would be filled with chapters that would bring anyone to tears. Their titles would be enough for *las lagrimas* to begin to fall.

Chapter titles for this very sad book:

"Missed Opportunities"
"Important Phone Calls I Never Returned"
"Important Phone Calls I Returned Too Late"
"My Second Chance Gone Bad"
"I Forgot to Follow Up and So I Fouled Up."

Yes, it's a book that will have its readers grabbing for a box of tissues with every turn of the page.

Perhaps a good book title is: *El Camarón Que Se Durmió.* "The Shrimp That Fell Asleep" would be based directly on a playing card from the game of *Lotería.*

The bright red shrimp waves its tentacles and appears to have the bright alert eye of someone "in the swim" of things. The little creature seems to be waving his arms frantically as if to say, "Hey you, wake up! Take advantage of opportunity."

But, when it comes to leaping at chances, I have been my own worst *enemigo* with no one to blame but myself. Missed opportunity. A second chance gone bad. Unreturned phone calls. Forgetting important dates.

All of our lives are littered with these poisonous failings that slow us down and cloud our future.

I am in counseling, therapy that is helping me to deal with the trauma of covering the World Trade Center attacks. In addition to helping me cope with the post-traumatic stress, my therapist, Dr. Barbara Grande is helping me to discover other issues on which I need to work.

One of those discoveries is that (and it is an issue with which I am still dealing) I can get a phone call or e-mail message that is brimming with promise and potential. Someone calling about a speaking engagement, a fun party to which I am invited, or perhaps a job possibility I should check out.

And there that message sits and sits *and* sits. My message light blinks on and off with an angry squint of resentment. I am once again letting opportunity pass me by. My e-mail sings "You've got mail" to an unresponsive audience.

Why? Why do I hold back, hesitate to return that phone call or respond to that e-mail that was so full of potential when it arrived at my doorstep?

Through years of playing the game of *Chalupa*, the importance of *El Camarón* escaped me.

Whenever the colorful, slightly creepy-crawly *Camarón* surfaced, we simply regarded its image as just another playing card, another stepping stone toward winning the latest round of Mexican bingo.

We didn't know at the time, but even then, while playing the game, we subconsciously absorbed the importance and true meaning of this valuable Chalupa Rule. In the heat of the game we had to stay alert and on our toes. We had to stay awake in order to not get swept away by the current of the game.

Camarón que se duerme se lo lleva la corriente. If you fall asleep, the current will sweep you away.

If the shrimp of our Chalupa Rule pauses for even a small moment in its lifetime of swimming, if it suspends its forward motion for one minuscule heartbeat of *camarón* time, then its defenses are down, its potential to survive diminishes. Its possibilities, in an instant, are cut down to zero. It falls asleep and is swept away by the current/ *la corriente.*

There have been many times when I have returned the call too late. I lost a stand-up gig because by the time I called all the performance slots were filled. And sometimes I don't respond to a party invitation until the function is over.

The more I delay in returning calls, the more they pile up, threatening me with their sheer numbers until I just decide to make them invisible. Maybe that way, they will just go away.

But why do we do this? As for myself, I think it's because if I don't answer that phone call or act on an offer then I really haven't been rejected. I let the possibility just hang there in the water, still and lifeless. Opportunities have swum right by me because I was too afraid to find out if they were really going to come true.

But when, like the *Camarón* of this Chalupa Rule, I fall asleep, very unpleasant things begin to happen. I get more nervous about the prospect of being rejected.

I worry about the eventual outcome and get distracted from the responsibilities of my daily routine. This *camarón* is about to get eaten up by the pressures of life. I get swept away by the current and others take advantage of my lack of action, my indecisiveness.

Let's be real about something. *¿Eres flojo?* Are you lazy? Don't let your fear or *pereza* get the best of you. Do what I did, admit it, and then move on. Denial of your laziness is not going to cure the problem. The first step is admitting it. Yes, I am lazy. I would rather sit on the sofa watching television than follow up on possibilities. I would rather take a nap than spend some time on the computer researching a new career path.

But then it hits me, this lazy *camarón* is forgetting one very important thing.

At least our generation of Latinos has opportunities to which we can swim. Our relatives, our aunts, uncles, grandparents, and older cousins were, in many ways, denied the chance to dip even one toe in the waters of hope and opportunity. Faced with discrimination and poverty, they had to float on the sidelines while only chosen *camarónes* were allowed the chance to swim toward the prize.

How dare I squander opportunity? They would have jumped at the chance to utilize their intelligence, talents, and skills to the fullest. Many never got that chance. By taking no action, I do them a disservice and tarnish their memory.

Now, this *camarón* jumps into the ocean of possibility, *patas primero* and asks questions later.

Admittedly, this is a Chalupa Rule that tests me every single day. Slowly but surely, I am working on conquering its challenges.

I have a special notepad where I write down all my messages from my home phone, my cell phone, and my calls at work.

As I return each call, I draw a line through the message. As the finished phone calls increase in number, I get a feeling of confidence that keeps me on track.

Another way we fall asleep in the current of life is through lack of follow-through. Someone mentions an opportunity that we should look into, we nod a halfhearted yes, and promptly forget all about it.

Post-it notes can save the day. As soon as I can, I put the information on a Post-it and stick it right on my computer screen and I don't remove it until I have done something about it. You can't work on a computer screen that's plastered with paper. Don't remove a note until it's taken care of.

I leave messages for myself on my voice mail. This makes me feel as if I have an assistant reminding me to make important calls.

I e-mail myself, also reminding myself to take action.

Also, I tell my family and friends about the opportunity as soon as I can. Yes, there is a risk that it won't pan out, but their friendly urging to check it out is more than enough impetus to keep on swimming in the waters of success. Just remember if you are going to confide in someone, choose carefully. You still have to guard your little pile of beans, remember?

Lack of follow-through has sunk many a *camarón*. Follow-through has opened many doors of opportunity. Follow-through will make you stand out in the crowd of *camarónes* who, chancing upon opportunity, swim right on by instead. Follow-through—and this is a hard one for me—includes sending thank-you notes to people who have helped you, advised you, or in any way have provided insight and assistance in your life. These notes are remembered fondly and also mark you as someone who is "on the ball."

I buy a book of stamps and stick them in my wallet. I keep a box of blank note cards on my desk. The note doesn't have to be some long, *Don Quixote* epic. Just a simple, "Dear So-and-so, *mil gracias* for the advice. Please let me know if I can ever do anything for you. *Sinceramente,* Mario."

Yá, es todo.

Stick it in the mail and you're done. Swim away, little *camarón,* and get on with your day.

Keep in mind the power of this Chalupa Rule. When you swim by a job possibility, when you ignore a suggestion, or let a phone call go unreturned, you are sitting in the land of zero opportunity.

Example: Someone asks to see your résumé. You feel that it is inadequate, that you don't have enough experience for the job. You think there are hundreds of people out there much better qualified than you who will probably get the job anyway, so why bother? Sound familiar?

Well, if you let that résumé sit on your desk or in your purse, it is sitting in the land of zero opportunity. Just by handing it in, you increase your opportunity hundreds of times. If you spend extra time polishing up that résumé (remember *Dale chine?*) you increase it thousands more.

Which would you rather have? Zero? Thousands? See what I mean?

I can already feel that a lot of *camarónes* out there are swimming a little more vigorously now.

This Chicano *camarón* almost missed out on the opportunity of a lifetime, a life-changing job, because I was almost too lazy to get up off my you-know-what and check something out.

In 1979, I was working as a general assignments reporter at KSAT 12 television in San Antonio, Texas. One Saturday, I was assigned to reporting duty. This is a generally slow time in the newsroom where you sit making phone calls, trying to develop a story.

I noticed on a television monitor that something interesting was going on. There was an audition. I turned up the volume and learned the audition was for a new television show called *PM Magazine.* The station was looking for local co-hosts.

Then, the moments of agony as this nervous *camarón* wrestled with a dilemma. At that moment, I became a confused combination of *pollo recién comprado* and a sleepy shrimp about to miss the opportunity of a lifetime.

Should I or shouldn't I? It was slow in the newsroom but breaking news could happen at any moment.

True to how I had been taught at home, your job comes first. But still, I felt I could do this job and I wanted to try.

A simple solution made it possible for me to audition. Instead of letting this chance slip by I went to the assignments manager and asked if I could be excused to audition for this show.

With the green light, I tried out. For the next seven years I was co-host of the show, I had incredible adventures and traveled to exciting parts of the world.

There was an opportunity and I swam toward it with the voices of so many relatives ringing in my ears. *No te duermas.* Don't fall asleep.

I will never fall asleep in the water again.

Camarón Que Se Duerme, Se Lo Lleva la Corriente

He Who Falls Asleep Will Be Swept Away by the Current

CHALUPA RULE SEVENTEEN

17

EL CORAZÓN
The Heart

I Never Eat Other People's Heartaches for Breakfast

Nunca Desayuno con los Pesares de Otras Personas

Prontito:

We all need to go on a special diet. This nutritional plan would eliminate one of the most dangerous food groups known to man: gossip. This toxic substance clogs the arteries of communication with hurt feelings and confusion.

Unfortunately, it's highly addictive. Many find it almost impossible to resist nibbling at other people's tragedies. Don't eat someone else's heartaches for breakfast.

A Lo Largo

You know the look. Someone is telling the story of some-one's problem, downfall, or scandal either at school, on the job, or in their personal life. There are a million variations to the tales but they all focus on the same thing; someone's un-fortunate experience is the main attraction.

Did you see it? There it is again. As they tell you the story (okay, let's be real . . . it's really gossip) you catch the tiniest hint of a smile on their face as they reveal it all, detail by gory detail.

There it is again. This time there is no mistaking it. Yes, they are actually smiling while they tell you the story.

The scene usually goes something like this:

"Hey did you hear what happened to Julio? Management caught him stealing copy paper from the supply room. Every-body says he's going to be terminated. Can you believe it? Isn't it awful?"

Or, the story can take on this type of flavor:

"Well, it's official. Gloria is going to break up with Ramiro today. Boy, is he going to be messed up after that. Serves him right. Can you believe it? Isn't it awful?"

"Isn't it awful?" I've been known to tell people, "If it's so awful then why are you smiling?"

In some way, even if they don't know it themselves, they are eating at the table of someone's misfortune. It seems inno-cent when you talk about it in terms like:

"Ay, we're just talking. We're not hurting anybody."

"It's just words. We're just having a little fun."

"We're not going to spread it anymore. We'll keep it to ourselves."

Innocent words, sure enough. But let's change the picture just a bit. Picture a big, fancy banquet table. However, instead of food and drink laid out for people to enjoy, imagine the following scene:

Instead of a big roast and accompanying dishes of vegetables, picture someone's family pictures, their résumé, and perhaps their husband or wife's photograph. On the same table, place big boxes labeled "Private" or "Personal" or "Confidential."

Instead of knives and forks, set the table with chainsaws and wood-chipping machines. Turn on the machines, fire up the chainsaws, and go at it. Tear up their family photos; don't forget the children and their *abuelitas*. Feed their résumés and other career-related material into the wood-chipper, smile as all of their most personal and vital information is shredded to tiny scraps of meaningless paper. Listen to the loud, roaring sounds of the chainsaws and the chippers as they go about their work of destroying someone's life.

Now, imagine yourself sporting a small, yet unmistakable smile while you go about your work.

When we eat someone's heartache for breakfast, we take bites out of their lives and use them to nourish our idle curiosities and fill the spaces of empty time that populate our days.

"Well, they deserve it. They shouldn't have gotten themselves into that mess if they didn't want people to talk about it," some people might answer. Well, there is another *dicho* that addresses that very comment. It's an old proverb, dusty with age and a little arthritic in the joints due to its very long life, but it still applies.

No escupas para arriba porque te puede caller en la cara.

This *dicho* may seem a little crude but there is no mistaking its insightful truth.

Don't spit upward because it may fall on your face.

Get it? A little bit of karmic return is evident in this old Mexican proverb.

It may take a few seconds, or perhaps a few years, but some of those words that are flippantly tossed around like a big *ensalada* may wind up on your face somewhere along the way.

None of us, absolutely none of us are strangers to gossip.
El chisme.
El bochinche.
Gossip.
We either spread it or we (sometimes unwillingly) hear it.
Gossip is a very adaptable, extremely versatile food item.
Chisme comes in a can:
"Someone told me not to say anything but it's been a few months since it happened so I figure I'm gonna go ahead and talk about it now."
Spill the *frijoles.*
Bochinche comes sizzling hot:
"Raul told me not to say anything, but he pissed me off so forget him. Listen to this."
Watch out. Hot plate.
Murmuraciones come ice cold:
"I overheard someone talking about Sara's money problems. I don't like her anyway so here goes."
Brrr. It's cold. Bundle up.
Gossip comes as fast food:
"Come here quick. I just found out. Dolores is pregnant. Nobody knows who the father is." Gobble gobble.
And as I mentioned before, gossip is also available as a sumptuous feast of many varied courses:
"I know I already told you about Dora's family problems. One more little story is not going to hurt anything. You see, all that is the least of her problems, now her son is on probation."
Pass the salt.
If you decide to snack on someone's misfortune keep this saying in mind: *Si tienes trapo de donde te corten, no cortes.* My *tías* were especially fond of this *dicho* because of its direct, unvarnished truth. Basically it means, "If you have cloth from which people can cut out some gossip, don't cut into others' cloth."
I keep one thought in mind whenever I am tempted to break this Chalupa Rule. Just when I am about to open my

mouth and repeat some juicy *chisme*, I say to myself, "Never say anything behind someone's back that you won't also say to their face."

That usually stops me. However, if and when I do say something critical of someone, I make it a point to force myself to tell them to their face. It's only fair.

And if you are overcome with the temptation to share a deep, dark secret with someone, *un secreto pero bien privado*, beware. You are just asking for someone to eat your heartaches for breakfast. Here is why: I have the theory that everyone, no matter how hard they may try to be otherwise, is a leaky grocery bag.

That's right, a leaky grocery bag.

When you go to the *tienda* to get your food they always pack your purchases into either paper or plastic. These bags do a good job of holding everything in until you get home. But remember, they are designed to last only for so long. After a while, they fall apart, opening at the seams and developing gaping holes from which your groceries fall out onto the ground. We have all experienced chasing oranges, toilet paper, and tortillas down the street when we've taken too long to get home. Don't blame the bag. They are designed that way. They are not meant to last forever.

When it comes to gossip and *cuentos*, we should assume most people are the same way: leaky grocery bags, designed to spill their guts onto the *calle*/the street.

We fill them up with our stories and thoughts and expect all of that information to stay inside of them forever.

But we have all had this experience:

I was in the newsroom of a New York City television station talking with a coworker, an excellent communicator, professional and reliable.

The information I shared with this person was not earth-shaking, just a repetition of what I had heard about changes that were coming to the newsroom as a new manager entered the picture.

A few days later, I overheard this same person repeat the information to a group of coworkers. It went something like this, "I can't remember where I heard this, but big changes are coming to the newsroom."

I can't remember where I heard this? You better believe I shrank into the woodwork when I heard that. They heard it from *me*.

This person was a leaky grocery bag, not designed to hold information in forever. Perhaps the original intention was to keep the information inside, but somewhere along the way the source was forgotten and it all entered the public domain (thankfully without my name attached).

People can eat your heartaches for breakfast another way. You may confide in someone and they make a *promesa* not to tell a soul. What you do not know is that their wife, husband, or significant other is usually exempt from that promise. Their best friend might be thrown into the bargain as well. This starts the chain reaction of "information sharing" where, somewhere along the way, your groceries wind up rolling down the street of gossip and innuendo. All because, "Hey, *I* didn't make the promise; you did."

The worst case of eating someone's heartaches, someone's tragedy for breakfast, came during the horrors of September 11.

I covered part of the story at Bellevue Hospital, where many family members of victims gathered, hoping for word of their loved one. As we now know, few survivors were pulled from the rubble. At the time, however, families and friends were desperate to find the missing.

While I covered the story, someone rushed up to me with a computer printout, a supposed "list of survivors" and their conditions. A wave of hope rushed through the crowd as people surrounded the person holding the list. Using a strong dose of reporter skepticism, I asked to see the list of names.

Something wasn't right.

I asked to borrow the list for a moment and ran to the nearest print shop to make a copy. Studying it closely, I made a shocking discovery. Many of the names listed were fictitious. The conditions listed (written in Spanish) were horrifyingly cruel. I know the names were made up because buried in the pages of the thick printout were the names of celebrities, cartoon characters, and even presidents. The conditions, translated into English, read "Help me, I am burning" and other extremely disturbing entries.

Much of the list was a hoax and I reported it as such on the air. It was hard to control my feeling of sadness that someone, in the depths of such a tragedy, took the time to make up a list that gave false hope to so many desperate families.

They ate someone's tragedy for breakfast. We never found the source of the false information but I can only hope the perpetrators have realized the cruelty of their "prank."

This story brings home the point that there are people out there who would do such a thing. In between that extreme and the harmless gossip at the other end of the heartache spectrum is a breathtaking variety of rumor, *chisme,* and outright lies.

If you are going to lose patience in life over something, then let it be over gossip.

If someone asks you for information about a coworker, about their personal life, simply answer, "Go ask them."

If someone tries to confide something deep and dark about someone and you are not comfortable getting that information say, "Thanks but the less I know the better."

I deliver my standard lighthearted but nonetheless clear message this way:

"I don't know nuthin. I do my job and I go home."

Nunca Desayuno con los Pesares de Otras Personas

I Never Eat Other People's Heartaches for Breakfast

CHALUPA RULE EIGHTEEN

18

LA LUNA
The Moon

Consult Your Pillow

Consulta con Tu Almohada

Prontito:

Try to "consult your pillow" when you have a big decision to make. There's a special power about assigning a decision to your subconscious mind. "Consulting your pillow" is not a passive act. It involves an investment of time. If a large purchase is looking too good to be true, then consult your pillow and get back to the salesman tomorrow. That "good deal" gets repeated all the time.

A Lo Largo

"I can hardly wait to tell him off."

"That deal is so good, I can't pass it up."

These statements are miniature time bombs. You might as well juggle hand grenades. These statements and others like them carry the possibility to cause major turbulence in your life.

These dangerous sentences are stamped with a heart-racing, blood-pumping urgency that clouds reason and smashes logic into a pile of mushy, refried beans.

They make you feel like you should take action. Now.

This old *dicho* got a lot of use in my family. When a big decision needed to be made and no clear choice came immediately to the surface that's when a relative said, "Consult your pillow." It seemed as if you were putting off that big decision but instead you were giving yourself a gift: time to make a rational decision.

And it's not just any time you are talking about. You will let your subconscious mind take over the decision-making process, all of this while you sleep.

I find it works especially well if, just before you fall asleep, you tell yourself what it is you want your *almohada* to consult. I have found that in the morning there is newfound clarity.

I have even tested it out. Just before going to sleep, I will say to myself, "wear the red tie tomorrow." More often than not, one of the first *pensamientos* that comes to my mind on awakening is the thought of the red tie. Try this experiment and see if it works for you.

By saying, "I will consult my pillow," you give yourself permission to "minimize" the pending decision on the computer screen of your mind. That way, you can concentrate on the important activities of the day while your subconscious mind mulls over the options before you. This Chalupa Rule advises you to take at least one night to allow your subconscious mind to weigh the issue at hand without the distraction of everyday life clouding your vision.

"Let me consult my pillow" works great with car deals that salesmen swear, "Won't be good tomorrow."

It helps when you are faced with offers of gym memberships that will only be at this low price for two more days.

Just say, "Let me consult my pillow" and walk away.

I wish I had invoked the power of this Chalupa Rule many, many years ago. I was young and naïve to the ways of high-pressure salesmanship.

I walked into a car dealership just to see what was new and before you know it, I had traded in my Ford Granada for a brand-new and very expensive LTD Crown Victoria. I did not need the car. My old car was just fine. Worst of all, I did not need the higher monthly payment.

A friend studied the numbers and learned that all sorts of hidden costs and options wound up in the final invoice, a statement I neglected to read.

I spent the entire night waking up, running to the door, and wishing the car would just vanish from the driveway. It took an attorney to get my original car back and cancel the deal. All of that stress because I had not consulted my pillow.

The new car deal will be there tomorrow.

The cheap gym membership will be offered again in a month.

The once-in-lifetime wide-screen television sale will be repeated in just weeks.

Test it out. Scan the newspapers everyday for the *baratas* (that's what we call sales in South Texas). Keep a record. What you want always seems to be on sale, at a reduced price and at one-time only terms.

There is another facet to this Chalupa Rule that carries its own special power. That is the power to change your mind. We are always so afraid to invoke this power because we fear that people are going to see us as wishy-washy, unpredictable, and flighty. However if you are generally known as a responsible, level-headed person, there is no reason why you cannot occasionally say, "I have changed my mind."

Several years ago, during contract negotiations, I had indicated a certain salary level that I would accept. After consulting my pillow and my calculator, I realized I needed more money. Before the talks went any further, I mentioned this change of situation. People were understandably surprised but I said, "I have changed my mind."

If used *con cuidado,* with care, this phrase provides some necessary breathing room when you are faced with *decisiones muy grandes.*

I have changed my mind.

Don't be afraid to use it.

What is the difference between these two phrases: "consulting your pillow" and "sleeping on it"? They seem be saying the exact same thing, but that is not the case. When you sleep on something it indicates an inactive state, a state of unconsciousness where nothing happens. When we "consult our pillows" we take an active role in the process. We open the gates for our subconscious mind to process the information while our body rests. It may seem like an insignificant difference, just "playing around" with words. However, I have learned there is power built into every single word we use.

So, when you say, "I am going to consult my pillow," you are energizing your mind to continue the decision-making process even while you rest.

There are times when we don't have a full-night's sleep to *consultar con tu almohada.* This Chalupa Rule can still work for you. Write down the issues at hand in as much detail as you can. Stick that list in your pocket and forget about it for an hour. At the end of that time period, pull out the list and read it. It feels as if someone else wrote the list and you are reviewing it from a third-person point-of-view. Now, you can be less emotionally invested in the decision and can come up with a sober, well-balanced answer.

You can even do a "microwave" version of this Chalupa Rule. On several occasions I have been upset at work or at home, flooded with emotion about either a professional or family issue. The urge is strong to "march right in there and give them a piece of my mind."

Primeramente, before you do anything, get a piece of paper and write down all the points that upset you. Go into as much detail as you can. Fold the piece of paper and stay away from it for at least five minutes. Put it in your purse or in a drawer.

Then, after the allotted time has passed, open up the paper and read it aloud. Nine times out of ten, some of the issues you thought were earth-shaking and extremely upsetting are really not. They are miscommunications that can be straightened out.

I have done this several times. On each occasion, after reading the list of my gripes, I breathed a sigh of relief that I did not speak out on all the points on the list.

Gracias a Dios.

Yes, some strong issues may remain that really need to be addressed, but at least you have sifted out those that are not as pressing.

This quick consulting of the pillow can save you a lot of discomfort and embarrassment when you are sorely tempted to "speak your mind."

There is one important factor involved in consulting your pillow. You have to get a good night's sleep to do it. So many times, our heads hit that *almohada* so full of stray thoughts and *preocupaciones* that the worries and restlessness prevent us from properly consulting our pillows.

For help with that sleepy problem I had to look no farther than my dog, Huitzi. You might remember him from Chalupa Rule Number Six, "Swim in Your Culture." Huitzi, a graduate of the Humane Society of New York, had to deal with several health problems including cancer, a collapsed trachea, and an open heart valve.

Despite all of his *problemas,* when bedtime arrived, Huitzi found a comfy spot in bed, breathed a sigh of relief, closed his eyes, and dropped right off to sleep.

Formerly abandoned, thirteen-year-old Popocateptl Tlaloc

Cuautemoc Quetzalcoatl Huitzilopochtli Paricutin Cutirinicuaro Bósquez Alcalá the Third hit the pillow and entered
doggie-dreamland before you could say *Ay Chihuahua.*

So, I now take my cues from him. I try to sleep like a dog. I
try to train myself so when I go to bed, I shut off the worries
and concerns of the day and assign them to my pillow.

That was another problem I had with properly consulting
my pillow. The same may go for you.

According to recent studies, Latinos have a shockingly
high incidence of a serious sleep disorder. We think we are
sleeping at night, *roncando,* snoring to our heart's content,
think that we are sleeping with *los angelitos.*

Think again.

We know about diabetes and Latinos. Serious. Now learn
about sleep apnea and Latinos. Serious.

For as long as I could remember, every morning I woke up
exhausted, as if I had never slept. Sleep with the *angelitos* indeed.

A television interview with an expert on sleep disorders
changed my life. I decided to do a story on snoring and spent
the night at a sleep clinic. They covered my body in sensors
and wires to get an accurate read of my sleep patterns. I
looked like a giant, electric tamale ready to bake all night.

The researchers discovered, to my shock, that during the
night I woke up over 200 times! In effect, I was not sleeping at
all. The diagnosis, sleep apnea, means your breathing stops
several times during the night. It causes loud snoring, and
puts some at the risk of death.

Es algo muy serio.

I admit that I now wear a CPAP mask when I sleep. That's
a device that delivers "Continuous Positive Airway Pressure."
It keeps the breathing pathways open so you can sleep safely
and soundly.

Now, I sleep like a baby and can say, with all assurance, that
I definitely consult my pillow every single night.

My subconscious is putting in a lot of overtime lately.

Consulta con Tu Almohada

Consult Your Pillow. Sleep on It

CHALUPA RULE NINETEEN

19

EL BORRACHO
The Drunkard

Leave the Bottle or Leave Us in Peace

Deja la Botella o Dejanos en Paz

> ***Prontito:***
>
> This is a tough, heartbreaking situation for any family, a problem that cannot be ignored. It must be addressed. Now. Today. Before it's too late. Explore all avenues of help and counseling. Do your best to help your family member with love, understanding, and nurturing. But if the problem is out of control and there is violence involved, then it's time to do something drastic.
>
> That person needs to find a new place to live so that the children can have peace of mind and grow up without the scars of an alcohol-impaired lifestyle.

A Lo Largo

This is the most difficult Chalupa Rule. I created it. It deals with drinking and family. I am very sorry if in life you had the misfortune of drawing this card. This card is destructive, it can tear your family apart. If you drew this card, then you have a tough but necessary decision to make.

Act carefully and don't wait too long before you deal with this card, *El Borracho.* No names of real people will be used, no fingers will be pointed.

I cannot absolutely tell you what to do. I do, however, strongly suggest the course of action I had to take: expelling that person from the family. This chapter chronicles that experience and offers the reasons why this is a viable course of action. Read it carefully and then decide if you must also throw *El Borracho* out of the house.

The challenge, how do you deal with a chronic drinker who threatens to destroy an entire family? The Chalupa Rule I had to use to help my family survive was to ask this person to live elsewhere.

There was a *borracho* in my family. As a matter of fact, there were many *borrachos* just about everywhere you looked. All of them were men, all of them were breadwinners, the main financial support of their families. Many of them looked like this card only a few times a year, an occasional payday when a lapse in judgment could be forgiven, or perhaps a wedding reception where the communal beer keg offered a limitless, foamy escape from the daily pressures of raising a family on lots of hard work but very little money.

But sometimes, unfortunately, someone in your life acts like *El Borracho.* It only takes so many Fridays of a wasted paycheck to devastate a family with unnecessary poverty and domestic violence.

Talk with the person who looks like this card. Get help for them, counseling, advice from their religious leader, their other family members, their friends.

If that is not enough, there is one more step to take. I took that step and to this day I do not regret it and I would do it again if I had to do so. Ignore the pleas of their relatives and of others who would advise you to do otherwise. For the sake of the rest of the family, ask the person to live elsewhere. Continue to help them, exhaust all sources, but take care of the rest of your family.

If you are old enough to do so and can afford to support the family on whatever money you make, then take on the responsibility.

Scream. Yell. Call the police. Do whatever you want, but don't look back. I didn't.

I told you some of these Chalupa rules weren't going to be easy. However, I lived it, I did it, and you may have to do the same.

If this person straightens up their act for a year, then maybe. But don't be fooled, especially if domestic violence is part of the picture.

Ignore the pleas from his family members that may say *Pobrecito* and "He's all by himself now."

Tell them, "He is a big boy now. He can take care of himself very well. He's a much bigger boy than I was when he was drinking and carousing and spending the food money."

Tell them that. Then work hard, support your family, live a good life, and peace will reign in your house. Stay in touch with the person who resembles this Chalupa card. When it is time. When your family is in one piece, then reestablish contact. Not before. And I mean it.

You may disagree with me when it comes to this Chalupa card. I will not quarrel with you. Only know that these Chalupa Rules take into account the darkest times in my life when the contents of beer bottles threatened to drown my family in despair.

I took action and life improved. We may still have been poor, we may still have struggled, but it became a fair fight. Us against the challenges of the world. No one within our ranks was threatening to bring down the entire house of Chalupa cards.

As far back as I can remember, the problem of drinking in our family seemed to be centered on the weekend. During the week, hardworking people poured their energies into their jobs, rising early and coming home late. The pressures of raising a family must have been great along with the constant worries of making a few dollars from a low-paying job stretch enough to cover everyone's needs.

Relaxing on the weekend is a time-honored tradition for many. However, there was one problem in our family. Along with this binge drinking came the threats of domestic violence and hard-earned money spent in drinking and gambling.

The current statistics available from the American Liver Foundation's website seems to bear this out. Susan Manuel of their Los Angeles Chapter writes that Latinos are suffering a terrible fate at the hands of alcohol. Manuel says that when it comes to dying from cirrhosis of the liver, Latinos have the highest death rate. All this, she says, according to recent studies. She makes note that among factors that lead to this you can include the poverty levels of many Latino families in the United States.

There's more. Manuel reports that, according to the study by the National Institute on Alcohol Abuse and Alcoholism, Latino men seem to suffer from binge drinking, the trend that I noted in my family. They apparently drink more at one specific time rather than stretching it out over the week.

For our family, the image of *El Borracho* from the traditional game of Chalupa was very real and very painful to experience.

As I mentioned before, some of the Chalupa Rules involve family issues that, while uncomfortable to discuss, are vital for Latinos to address. This is one of them. The decision you make on how you handle your life if this Chalupa card is dealt to you is a completely personal and delicate one. No person from the outside, looking in, is going to offer you the perfect *remedio*. The solution, the remedy that you develop for your family comes after a long trip down the road of weighing all of your options, offering all of the help that is available and getting the understanding and acceptance of other family members and friends.

The reasons that people drink are varied and spring from so many sources that is impossible and unrealistic to discuss them here. There are, however, some reasons that I have heard in my own life that I would like to mention. The most universal reason goes something like this, "I drink because . . ." You can fill in the blank in countless ways. The ones that I have heard:

"I drink because my father drank."
"I drink because life isn't fair."
"I drink because your mother drives me to drink."
"I drink because I like it."

The only excuse from this list that I feel is the most valid, truthful one is the last one.

It is a reason I myself heard when I offered the heavy drinker in our family the opportunity to quit work and go back to school while I would take on the role of supporting the family.

Actually the reason went more like this, "I like to drink and gamble and nobody's going to stop me."

It was an honest response and one that compelled me to take action.

It was time for this person to leave the house, to go live somewhere else. Whatever financial burdens existed would fall on my shoulders and those of my sisters but so be it.

The choice was made. And I have never looked back.

Yes, there was resentment in parts of the family as to how I could do such a thing to a fellow family member. Yes, there were tremendous financial problems. But again, peace reigned in the house. You may like to drink but you can't do it here.

To this day, I do not drink. I cannot say I will never sip a glass of wine or perhaps taste a beer but I sincerely doubt it. I have seen enough of the tremendous damage that alcohol can do: financial damage, emotional damage, and even spiritual damage. That is enough for me to skip the drinking. It has not come without its pressures.

"Hey, you don't drink. Are you some kind of former alcoholic or something?"

"Here, have just one. One isn't going to hurt you."

"Come on. You have to drink wine with this dinner."

There is a simple reply to all of the above.

"No thank you."

Alcohol in moderation is something with which many Latinos feel comfortable. But in my opinion, any concerned Latino parent worried about teenaged drinking should not have a fully stocked bar in the house or several six-packs cooling in the refrigerator. Many statistics bear out a painful fact, that drinking in Latino households causes a large share of misery and if the family is also poor, only aggravates the situation.

Many people say they drink, or use drugs for that matter, because they were hurt deeply somewhere along the way. Perhaps it was a relationship gone bad, a tough childhood, or perhaps a parent or other older relative who drank. This is the source of one of those drinking excuses: "I drink because . . ."

I cannot presume to get into anyone's head or life. I can only speak from personal experience so please take what I am about to tell you with that firmly in mind.

Here is an example I always use when I speak to young Latinos at school events. The topic is usually the issue of growing up in poverty and then using that as a reason to check out of life and not work toward a goal. The analogy is this: Say that at the age of six you break your arm. The arm is put into a cast until it heals. Then, a few months later, that cast is removed and the healing process continues.

The point is, the cast is removed and the healing process continues.

Later in life, at the age of thirty-six for example, it's a pretty safe bet that you are still not wearing the same arm cast you were wearing at the age of six. The cast was removed. Except for perhaps hurting when the weather changes, the arm has healed.

This is the same in many ways with bad experiences that happen early in life. It has happened. Many, many times you have healed and still, years later, you use it as an excuse not to further your life. If it has not healed, get help. Therapy is a valuable way to face the past and stop it from haunting your present and endangering your future. Your church, if you belong to one, is another way to get counseling. And, if there is no money, contact local organizations that offer free therapy and counseling. Drinking should not be used as a "permanent cast" plastered to whatever hurt or problem you have.

In addition, if there is strong evidence that drinking is a pattern in your family and that alcoholism is a big risk, don't drink at all.

Don't drink at all.

If you are a parent who drinks and has problems with alcohol read this very carefully, as children remember.

Later in life when they are adults, they will recall all the heartache and the sorrows that problems with drinking bring upon a family. This is a problem that can shatter a family, the reverberations lasting for the rest of your life.

This is the best way to avoid the heartbreaking tragedy of this Chalupa card.

If you need help, get it. If someone needs help, get it
for them. Don't ignore this Chalupa Rule.

Deja la Botella o Dejanos en Paz

Leave the Bottle or Leave
Us in Peace

20

LA DAMA
The Lady

Everyone Needs a Diana Rodríguez

Todo el Mundo Necesita una Diana Rodríguez

Prontito:

Do you know someone who is too scared to get out on the dance floor of life? Then they may need a little prodding to get into the thick of things. You can be someone's "Diana Rodríguez," their catalyst to help make their dream come true. If you see potential in someone, help them to develop it. Be their inspiration, their muse. They will eventually thank you for it.

A Lo Largo

I was in the eighth grade. It was the spring dance. I was dying to get out on the dance floor. But I was paralyzed; I couldn't move and was too terrified to ask any girl to dance. I was doomed to spend the entire evening standing on the sidelines with the other *caguías* (which is a-not-very-nice Tex-Mex way of saying chicken shit).

Suddenly, I felt the strong grip of someone grabbing me by the arm and pushing me toward the dance floor. I couldn't see the person's face and I was too stunned by the bold action to resist.

We got out in the middle of the dance floor and I finally looked into the face of the person who had landed me in the middle of all those dancing couples, where I really wanted to be in the first place. That person was Diana Rodríguez, easily the most beautiful girl in the eighth grade at Tafolla Middle School on the west side of San Antonio, Texas. I remember Diana saying, "I could tell you really wanted to dance, well now you are."

And that was that. She changed my life. I had learned to take charge of situations where I felt helpless and was desperate to take action. However, sometimes in life someone just needs to come in and grab you by the arm and take you where you really wanted to go in the first place. You must be open to the experience.

There have been many Diana Rodríguezes in my life. These are people who see something in you before you see it yourself. They may sense an ability, a skill, or a talent of which you may not be aware yourself. Let them guide you to your talent. Let them be your Diana Rodríguez, as my "handcrafted" rule advises.

This is a dual-purpose card for the Chalupa Rules. Also, in life you need to be someone's Diana Rodríguez. If you pick up on someone's dreams or desires, if you sense their talent, then help them on the way. They may need to be grabbed and pushed onto the dance floor of life. Take them by the arm and walk them right into the middle of where it's happening. When the opportunity presents itself, take charge and become someone's Diana Rodríguez.

The concept of this Chalupa Rule has served me well so far. This rule turns on a special searchlight in your mind as you become more aware of others' hopes and dreams. Becoming sensitive to others' plans and blueprints for the future will, in turn, make you more attuned to your own.

When someone feels enough trust and confidence in you to reveal their dreams and desires, many times they are at a crossroads in their life.

They are faced by the big, "Walk, Don't Walk" sign at the intersection and for some reason theirs is stuck on "Don't Walk."

They trust you enough to reveal their plans to you. You have quite a bit of enabling power at this point. With your encouragement and positive response, they may feel more green-lighted to go ahead with their passions and plans.

They are looking for a Diana Rodríguez. You can be their Diana Rodríguez.

There are standard responses that can work when you are being someone's Diana Rodríguez. You can say, "Go for it" or "You won't know how it works until you try it." However, you need to shine a somewhat brighter green light in their direction. Try the following:

Everyone knows from taking those junior high school classes in General Physical Science that electricity has certain properties to its nature. One rule is that electricity "follows the path of least resistance."

What this means is that when given a choice an electrical current will travel along a pathway that is the easiest, that makes the flow of its energy more efficient in its line of travel. It follows the path of least resistance.

I feel it is the same way with all the things we want to try in our lives and in our careers. We should follow that path of least resistance to reach our goals.

Here is how I define the path of least resistance. If working with computers comes easily to you, then follow that path of least resistance.

If people tell you that you give good advice and can always be counted on for being a fair, impartial listener then perhaps the path of least resistance for you is that of counselor or therapist.

If you notice that one of your children has what seems to be a natural knack for doing something, then perhaps that is their path of least resistance. In a friendly, loving, and non-pressuring way you can quietly become their Diana Rodríguez.

Although many people are self-starters, there are others—yours truly included—who need to be triggered into action. However, it takes a special person with keen insight in order to spot someone who really wants to get out there and dance.

You don't have to be a loud and obnoxious Diana Rodríguez.

Here are some examples:

When I was dying to try out standup comedy, a friend took on that role of quiet encouragement. Ray Parisi handed me a copy of the book *Zen and the Art of Standup Comedy*. I read the book and it led me down the path of least resistance for me, which was to try out standup comedy and see if I liked it.

Does making someone laugh come easily to you? Do people sometimes say, "Hey you should try standup comedy"? Then listen to what people are telling you. Many cities offer workshops in standup comedy technique. They also usually include a guaranteed spot at a local comedy club. Even if this doesn't launch you into a career that makes you the next Paul Rodríguez or George Lopez, at least you can say you tried it, you took the chance. You were your own Diana Rodríguez.

I would like to take this time to thank my very own Diana Rodríguez. I wish I had known at the time what a big difference she was going to make in my life.

There I was, this shy kid dying to get out in the middle of the dance floor. I had no idea that someone was there watching me, noticing my quiet distress. My Diana Rodríguez was perceptive enough to pick up on that and then take action.

If she hadn't taken me out to dance, I would have spent the entire evening anxious to dance but too shy to do anything about it.

I am sure that you have experienced the power of a Diana Rodríguez at some time or another in your life. That is when someone notices something in you and helps you to reach your goal. Hopefully, you have been someone's Diana Rodríguez and helped someone's dream come true.

I often wonder how I can find my Diana Rodríguez and personally thank her for what she did on that night of the school dance at Tafolla Middle School in San Antonio, Texas. This Chalupa Rule was among the very first to be included when I began to write this book.

I had tried very hard throughout my life to be someone's Diana Rodríguez. I looked for opportunities to kick-start someone's dream, to get them into the middle of the dance floor of their future.

I launched a search for my Diana Rodríguez. My first telephone call was to Tafolla Middle School. Although the person who answered the phone, Mrs. Chavez, was extremely helpful, she mentioned that there was no way to access school records from that time period. So, Diana Rodríguez from San Antonio, Texas, a former "Tafolla Toro," I want to thank you for grabbing my arm and leading me right out into the middle of that dance floor.

Todo el Mundo Necesita una Diana Rodríguez

Everyone Needs a Diana Rodríguez

CHALUPA RULE TWENTY-ONE

21

EL ÁRBOL
The Tree

Shake All the Branches

Sacude Todas las Ramas

Prontito:

Most opportunities don't fall into your lap. You shake all the branches by exploring all the possibilities that surround you. Don't blame God or the universe if good job prospects and golden opportunities don't float into your life. Take risks. Ask questions. Pick up the phone and make contact with experts in your field of interest. Make your own luck. Shake all the branches.

A Lo Largo

We make such a big deal about luck. We are lucky when this happens. We are fortunate when that takes place. I think you make luck happen.

If you walk in a straight line, eyes always locked forward, then your opportunities to find luck are as narrow as the road you take. Look to the sides as you walk your path. Take a look at all tree branches that hang overhead. Those tree limbs are literally dripping with opportunity, ripe for the plucking. But if you don't reach out and take your luck, nothing will happen.

You have to shake all the branches as you walk by those trees. We all despair when things don't happen to us, when someone else has all the luck. It seems as if God or the universe has forgotten us while it showers everyone else with good fortune, good career, and a happy life full of wonderful things.

Almost everything that has happened to me has taken place because I reached out and grabbed it. Yes, there have been wonderful, caring people who have extended the hand of assistance and for that I am forever grateful. But, if I had not grabbed hold of those helping hands and done something with what I was given, nothing at all would have happened.

There is a solid, necessary reason why we should shake the branches of life to see what falls out for us.

For example, in the workplace, this Chalupa Rule should be our everyday friend. As soon as we begin a new job we should look around the environment to see what other opportunities there are. That is not to say that you should be distracted from the important task of learning and mastering your new job. Rather, you should begin the process of sizing the place up, doing a systems check to see opportunities, finding what branches can be shaken later on in your career.

This way, you develop a goal, something to shoot for. The

minute a weight lifter picks up a fifty-pound weight, his or her mind is already on the sixty or seventy-pound barbell. That is why he picked up the lighter weight in the first place, so that he could prepare for and handle the heavier loads that are ahead.

The same goes for the rest of us. Shake the branches of your career environment and see what falls out for you.

That should also happen in school. What are your interests? What are your passions? What is there on campus that can fill that void for you?

Explore the clubs available. That is one way to shake the branches. Ask about special projects and classes that can satisfy that need for you.

At work, join organizations appropriate for your field: community groups, fundraising projects, and business clubs. In addition to helping and nurturing your community you also learn about other career possibilities in your field of interest.

If you sit at your desk and do your job well, then great. You will be recognized and perhaps given raises and promotions. However, if you reach out and shake the branches that are all around you, you multiply your chances a million-fold.

There is nothing more satisfying than holding in your hands something that you have made yourself. You can "handcraft" your future with opportunities you create.

Even if a certain lead or possibility seems remote and unattainable, go for it. Ask the questions. Request a job interview. Send the résumé and ask questions later.

At one point in my career, I looked for change, a way to revitalize my professional life. I was told that a certain television station did not have any openings but was interested in speaking with me about future possibilities.

I met with those in charge and, after one interview, had a job offer the very next day. If I had said, "No, I'll pass on that job interview. There's nothing there for me right now," then I would have missed out on a great opportunity.

If you have an idea for a special project at work then write your ideas down.

Get them into strong, presentable form. Request a meeting with your boss and present your idea. Even if it doesn't come to fruition you have already made yourself stand out as a self-starter, an innovator who is truly interested in the workings of the company. You are proving to your boss that you know how to "shake the branches" for new ideas.

You never know what is going to fall out of the branches you shake. It may not be what you expected, but it may surprise you. Take the risk to explore and create new opportunities that did not exist before.

When two film stars wanted to start their own television show, no one would give them a job. Television executives felt the U.S. public wasn't ready for their kind of marriage. If they would have stopped there then that's when their dream would have died. Instead, they went out and began shaking all the branches. They took their idea on the road, performing a stage version of their concept before live audiences, getting very positive reception. They proved their point to network executives. The show worked. The public was ready for a comedy about a Latino married to a *gringa*.

They did not stop. They shook the branches and made their own luck. Their dream did not fail. *I Love Lucy* was born.

Sacude Todas las Ramas

Shake All the Branches

22

LA MÁQUINA DE ESCRIBIR
The Typewriter

May You Always Be Self-Correcting

Que Siempre Seas Auto-Corregible

Prontito:

   The best work-related compliment that someone can pay you is that you are "self-correcting." This indicates you are a "self-monitoring" person, able to step outside of yourself to assess your performance. If change is necessary you are able to put it into motion without waiting for someone to tell you.

A Lo Largo

The nicest work-related compliment I ever received came from a news director who said he never worried about me or my work because he felt I was self-monitoring and self-correcting. What he meant is that whenever I made a mistake on the air or developed a problem with delivery that needed work, I addressed the problem myself before he had to say anything.

This Chalupa Rule deals with this concept, that you should always be your own best monitor and self-correcting of your work.

Do not always wait for others to say something.

Some of you may not recall some old electric typewriters that were very popular just before computers entered the picture. They were called IBM Selectric Typewriters, and when they hit the market we thought they were the next best thing to Mami's enchiladas. If you made a mistake, all you had to do was back up, hit the self-correcting key and the machine typed over the mistake. Just like that.

Ay Dios mío. Que milagro.

These self-correcting machines were time-saving wonders.

When that news director made that comment about me, the very first image that popped into my mind was one of those typewriters, always capable of fixing their own mistakes.

So, my image for this has always been the IBM Self-Correcting Typewriter.

We should all have, inside ourselves, a system that makes us self-correcting, always monitoring ourselves for ways that we can improve without having always to be told to do so.

I always try to be like an IBM
self-correcting typewriter.

Que Siempre Seas Auto-Corregible

Always Be Self-Correcting

23

LA RISA
Laughter

If at First They Laugh . . .

Si Primero Se Ríen . . .

Prontito:

Many times, when you present your thoughts and ideas to someone, their first reaction is to grin or laugh. This can shock you into hiding your creative thoughts and keeping your plans to yourself, inside where they often fade into oblivion. You have to learn to "survive the laughter." There *is* acceptance on the other side.

People mean well; it's just that your idea is new to them and the human reaction many times is to smile and/or laugh. They are not making fun. They are making room for the idea in their head. Survive the laughter, ride it out like a friendly wave in the surf. Keep your ideas alive.

A Lo Largo

This Chalupa Rule can help conquer a great killer of dreams. It has destroyed billions of bright ideas, countless new concepts, and innumerable inventions.

This experience has touched us all with its ability to pour corrosive acid on any idea or concept that we may have been nurturing privately. Think back, it could have happened to you years ago or it could have taken place yesterday. Either way, the effect is just as devastating to your self-esteem and to your confidence.

This great destroyer of dreams can strike at home, in school, and especially at the workplace. When it happens to you, there is no mistaking that sinking feeling in the pit of your stomach that signals "Abandon ship" or more precisely "Abandon dream."

You have an idea, a dream, or perhaps a grand plan. You get brave enough to expose your dream to the harsh light of day, hoping for some glimmer of validation, a thimbleful of encouragement.

And then it happens. You look closely at the face of the person or persons at whose feet you've just laid your precious dream for inspection and approval. You could swear there is a smile of encouragement blooming across their face. But that smile evolves into something else—a wide grin accompanied by a big dose of laughter. It might as well be a sharp knife in your heart.

You recover quickly, or try to anyway.

The sequence goes something like this:

You: "Hey, I have this great idea."

Coworker: "Oh really, what is it?"

You: "I think I can streamline our office procedures, that way we can save time and money for the company."

Coworker: (Wide grin. Laughter.) "You? You're not even a manager. Do you think they are going to listen to you? You're wasting your time."

You: "You're right. It was just a dumb idea, I guess."

End of scene.

End of dream.

I know this scene or something very much like it sounds familiar to you.

When, as a child, you open your mouth to sing and someone laughs.

When you show your drawing to a grown-up and they laugh at how silly your artwork is, you either hide it in a drawer or throw it away.

This dream killer can be overcome. You can create systems within yourself so that you survive the laughter. Sometimes though, it is not laughter at all. Instead it's a subtle little smile on someone's face that indicates your idea is silly and not worth the effort. But either way, if it's outright "Ha Ha" or simply that dream-killing sneer, it can stop your dreams in their tracks.

But you can survive the laughter if your prepare yourself. First you have to do some exercises to make yourself strong, to get yourself ready for when you bring your plans and ideas to light.

Try this exercise. It will serve two purposes. One, it will train you to "survive the laughter" when you mention an idea to someone. Second, it will make you brave enough to express your thoughts without fear of ridicule. With a serious look on your face and with absolute conviction in our voice, tell a friend or family member something like this: "Hey, I think I'm going to run away and join the circus. I am going to become a professional clown." That should get them laughing right away. Listen closely to the laughter. It is exactly the same laughter you hear when you tell someone your dream, aspiration, or plan. Train yourself to survive that response. Ride the waves of laughter like a surfer and remember where it is coming from: shock and surprise. Sometimes, however, their laughter comes from some "not-so-good-places": derision, envy, or jealousy.

Oh, and remember to tell them you are just kidding about the circus clown plans.

There is a vital point to make about this Chalupa Rule: it is most toxic to children. We should exercise *mucho cuidado* when a child tells us their hopes and dreams. They are looking to us for approval and they will forever remember our reaction.

One time as a young boy, I was laughed at, yelled at, and almost struck, all because an adult male member of our family saw me in the street, holding a violin. I wasn't interested in playing the violin, it simply belonged to a neighbor friend who was showing it off to her playmates. The violent reaction I received when I got back inside the house sent a very clear message: Boys don't play the violin. That type of instrument is for sissies, so this young child never dared to entertain dreams of classical music training. That dream was killed in less than two minutes.

There is another way handle a child's need for approval. With great care, as if you are handling the most expensive *joyas* in the world. Those prized jewels are the seeds of their future, don't kill them before they have a chance to take root.

You might think that a little kid won't remember comments you make to them as children. Think again. I remember drawing a picture of an apple when I was a very young boy. This is a vivid memory, so strong that I can still recall the misshapen apple and red color from the crayon spilling way outside the lines. At that age, I thought I had done a pretty good job so I showed it to one of my aunts, waiting for her approval. "That is very good. It is the best." She used words to that effect, in her response to my artistic effort. One sentence is definitely burned in my brain, "It is the best." Even then, at the age of six or seven, I can remember thinking, "It's not that good." But either she saw something in the drawing that showed promise or she was very careful not to trample on a child's tender self-esteem. Her approval made me feel good. I ran back to the coloring book and the box of crayons, happy that an adult had responded well to my work.

Four decades later I can still remember that moment. But in that same amount of time I can still remember the times when someone laughed at me, at my attempts to sing, at my desire to enter the world of broadcast journalism, and at my ethnicity. But I survived that laughter and was able to fashion a Chalupa Rule that I can now share with you.

I can still remember the waves of laughter from some relatives when I asked an aunt for a cutting from one of her flowering plants. I had a small garden in the backyard and I wanted to add that plant to my collection. Again, boys aren't supposed to do that. Well, this boy did and I continued with my garden, growing carrots, tomatoes, and flowers. To this day, I have a garden in my New York City apartment full of orchids, palms, and ivies. If I had let that laughter kill my love of plants, I would not be able to enjoy them today.

Sometimes we make people laugh without even knowing it. If we are not careful we can misinterpret that laughter, sending our thoughts in the completely wrong direction.

My first few days as a television reporter in New York City were full of terror, nerves, and uncertainty. Was I doing a good job? Were they ready to ship me back home, disappointed in my work? Was this the day I would fumble a story and get fired?

Those fears almost became a reality during the first few weeks on the job. Working as the Long Island correspondent for a New York television station, I had been assigned to a story in Mineola, Nassau County.

Heading toward the story with photographer Alan Horowitz, I realized that I had absolutely no money in my pocket. Thankfully, Alan also revealed that his pockets were empty as well.

Trying to make a good impression on this big-time New York City cameraman, I lunged out of our unmarked news vehicle and ran up to the ATM. The machine spat out the twenty dollars (my food budget for the week, by the way) and I dashed back, jumping into the car for the big "getaway."

The problem is that I jumped into the wrong car. So worried about making a good impression, I didn't even look up at the vehicle before entering. There I was, sitting in a stranger's car. The person in the driver's seat was shocked beyond belief that a television reporter jumped into the car with them. I looked back and Alan was howling with laughter, pounding the dashboard and trying to catch his breath.

I exited the car, apologizing profusely. I opened the door to the news unit and gales of laughter poured out. Alan, trying to catch his breath, wheezed out, "I can't believe you did that!"

Humiliated beyond words, I simply smiled and looked straight ahead, certain that "Mario is an idiot" would be the catch-phrase for me. What a way to start a brand-new job.

It could have gone the other way. I could have remained uncomfortable and expressed annoyance at being "laughed at." Instead, I rolled with the punches and managed to laugh at myself. The incident broke the ice between Alan and me, and the friendship has lasted for many years.

Remember that first burst of laughter can be unsettling, it's like a speed bump that rattles your nerves and shakes your confidence. Hang tight until you figure out exactly what is making someone laugh.

There are moments when someone's laughter or snicker can hurt you deeply. That is also a crucial time to survive the laughter.

I am always humbled and deeply honored when I receive an award. The awards ceremony at which the recognition is presented is always a touching and unforgettable experience. Unfortunately, due to my mother's illness, she was never able to attend any of the New York City ceremonies. On November 19, 1999, the City Council of New York honored me during their

Hispanic History Month celebration. My sisters Irene and Susanna were able to attend, as well as my niece Alexandra.

During my acceptance speech, I told the audience that I had my cell phone and was going to make a special phone call, to my mother who was unable to attend due to serious illness. I held the cell phone into the air and my mother heard the entire presentation, her spirit there in the room with us.

Those present received this special guest warmly and even cheered my mother as she listened. However, the next day at work, while walking by a small group of people, I overheard comments about "Mario's cell phone" at City Hall. I could detect a note of humor in the voices. Instead of allowing that to spoil my family's moment, I walked away without ever letting anyone know that I had heard them.

It was more than enough that my mother, in her own way, was present at City Hall in New York City on that special night. I survived the laughter again and a precious memory lives on.

There is another facet to this Chalupa Rule. You have a job to do if you want to follow its spirit to the letter. Be prepared when someone approaches you and says, "I have something I want to tell you." Keep in mind that they have probably been agonizing over whether to share their idea or plan with someone. For reasons that perhaps only they will ever know, you are the chosen one. At this point, I feel people become impressionable children once again, their self-esteem delicate and easily bruised. Even the most patient and understanding of us can be broadsided by what sound like outlandish, unrealistic thoughts and schemes that our friends and family can hatch.

While it's important to help them see the positive and negative side of any plan or idea, at the outset it's also vital to validate their right to dream and to dream big. The world isn't varied and unique because someone is inventing and reinventing sliced bread over and over again. It's the difference that makes the difference. The world is run on ideas that at first seemed silly or ridiculous, so hear them out.

When someone presents an idea for your review, restrain that snicker, hold back that twitch of the lip that can mean derision, and most of all, don't laugh.

The best response is to say, "Oh really, that sounds interesting. Tell me more." It comes as quite a relief when someone cushions your creative process with understanding and patience. You can help someone survive the laughter.

People are going to laugh. You can count on it. It's human nature. Take this book for example.

Gracias a Dios for this Chalupa Rule, otherwise it never would have come into existence. Someone would ask me about the book and I would launch into an explanation. Then, the big question, "What is the title of the book?"

Well, it's called *The Chalupa Rules*. Cue the laughter. Cue the snickers. Every time that happens I strap myself in and go along for the ride. Once the reaction subsides, I patiently explain what the book is all about. Just about every time, people are captivated by the idea and I survive the laughter once again.

Okay, at this point, it's time to be real about another aspect involving this Chalupa Rule. Sometimes your ideas and thoughts aren't quite ready for prime-time viewing. Maybe you are still hatching the concept and working out the bumps. In that case you should do what we did as a family when we were broke and didn't have enough money to buy something right away.

Put your idea on "layaway."

Growing up, "layaway" was an indispensable financial tool, just about the only one we had available to us if we wanted big-ticket items.

We went to the store, selected the items, gave a small down payment, and every month paid a little until the total was satisfied. The layaway purchases were ours to keep. Simple as that.

You can use the concept of layaway to keep your ideas under lock and key until they are ready for life on the "outside" of your brain, where they can survive the laughter. So, if you feel you need to hang on to an idea for a while, think to yourself, "It's on layway. Someday it will be out in the open and ready to put into operation."

This Chalupa Rule, *Si primero se ríen . . .* can save you hurt feelings and confusion at people's reactions to your thoughts and words. Boiled down to its simplest essence, this rule is very similar to the pattern people go through when something bad happens: shock, denial, and acceptance.

In the case of this Chalupa Rule, it's shock, laughter, and then acceptance.

Just keep in mind, there is usually acceptance on the other side of that roller-coaster ride of laughter. So strap yourself in, let your ideas fly, and survive the laughter.

Si Primero Se Ríen . . .

If at First They Laugh . . .

CHALUPA RULE TWENTY-FOUR

24

LAS TRENZAS
The Braids

Do What You Came Here to Do

A Lo Que Te Truje, Chencha

Prontito:

We spend too much time getting ready to get ready to get ready to work. We circle around a task, avoiding it and making up excuses to begin. *Jump* into work. Don't delay. Skip the preliminaries, the whining and complaining. Arrive on the job and begin to work. If you have homework to do, *do your homework.* Start work first and ask questions later.

A Lo Largo

¿*Chencha*? What kind of a name is that? It's probably short for Inocencia or Vicenta. But those are just wild guesses. I don't know. Is she make-believe? Is she a real woman from the pages of Latino history? Will Salma Hayek play her in a feature film one day? All those questions are in the land of *Yo no sé*. I don't know.

This woman, whoever she is or was, is part of my life. She prods me on a daily basis to get the job done without a lot of whining, complaining, and wringing of hands saying, "I'm tired" or "I'll finish tomorrow." No, if you listen to the *Chencha* of this Chalupa Rule, you'll get the job done fast and without a lot of, as my sisters say, "baby-crying."

I found confirmation for this very old *dicho* in something called, *El Diccionario Breve de Mexicanismos* by Guido Gómez de Silva. Translated, his interpretation says, "Do what I brought you here to do; let's not lose time." The phrase is not uncommon in South Texas and in Mexico.

Even though the definition is very helpful as the far as the meaning of the saying is concerned, it offers no clues as to who exactly this famous *Chencha* was in real life. No matter what, she lives on in Mexican history as the centerpiece of a proverb that all Latinos can use as they navigate life in the United States.

A lo que te truje, Chencha. Waste no time. Do what you came here to do. Don't even think about anything else. Just jump in and do the job.

This Chalupa Rule has helped me many, many times in life. Especially when the task is unpleasant, when a million different excuses exist for straying. This old proverb rings in my ears whenever I start a project or arrive for a day of work.

A lo que te truje, Chencha.

Now, let's be real. I have a big problem using and conquering the demands of this vital, extremely necessary Chalupa Rule. If the laundry needs doing, if there are shirts that need to be ironed, or if there is a work project that needs my attention, they always seem to wait while I watch TV, read a magazine, or do nothing at all. I absolutely have to trick myself in order to live up the challenge of this rule. Remember, it calls for you to skip all the preliminaries and jump right into work. That's right, *brinca* into work.

Observing the elders of the household in our busy, bustling Latino families brings home this way of thinking. All of our older relatives—the *tíos, tías, abuelitos,* and *abuelitas*—they never mess around. They get up. They have their *cafecito* and, after their cup of coffee, get right to work. They pick up the broom without one single whine or complaint. They head to work without the litany of *Ay Dios míos* that younger Latinos, me included, are so famous for doing.

What is their *secreto*? Is there a magic pill they take or some mysterious *brujería* they perform? No, there is no secret or magic spell. They are simply, whether they are aware of it or not, living by the spirit of this Chalupa Rule.

A lo que te truje, Chencha.

How can we jump into the heart of this Chalupa Rule? It's very hard but it can be done. I have some crazy yet very effective methods that work for me.

Housework. I select my favorite music and load up the stereo with the CDs. I decide on a job, sweeping for example. Find your favorite music and play it loud. Start a song and start a task at the same time. Dance around if you want to, but do the task while the song plays. When the song ends, see how much of the task you have performed. I promise it's a lot more than if you had just spent your time sitting down, twiddling your thumbs while the music plays. It is much easier to finish the job when you have the music of Marc Anthony, La India, or Luis Miguel filling your house.

If you are worried about the neighbors or the rest of the family then use a portable music device; put on the headphones and you'll get a big chunk of that sweeping done.

Also, it's not that *Chencha* doesn't want you to have fun.

She just wants to you save it for later. *Chencha* knows that there is plenty of time for relaxing moments but *después*, okay? I worked two jobs and went to school during my college years. I was a substitute teacher and worked in the electrical department at Sears and Roebuck on the south side of San Antonio. I had no choice. There was a family I had to help support. While I worked and studied my brains out I used to think about all the great nightclubs, restaurants, and movies that were absent from my life at the time.

I felt so sorry for myself sometimes. *Pobrecito de mí*, I used to think. Poor little me, I'm working while my friends are out partying and having a blast. Well, I did miss those great dinners, movies, and nights out dancing. But guess what. There are still restaurants, movies, and dance clubs in this world right now, this very day. They are still here for me to enjoy. They will be there for you as well; they aren't going anywhere.

Chencha is right. Work hard. There is time for fun later.

My mother knew that. She always said, "I will get all the hard work done first and then I can relax and enjoy myself without worrying about what I have to do."

She always kept her word. Mami would cook, clean, and sweep until the house was spotless. Then, when *all* the housework was done she would send me to the store for a Milky Way candy bar, a bottle of Coca-Cola, and a *True Detective* magazine.

While we took our afternoon siesta or read a book, our mother made herself comfortable and snuggled up with her one guilty pleasure of the day, her work done, her mind and body at rest.

She lived up to the saying *A lo que te truje, Chencha* by working hard and rewarding herself at the end of her duties.

That's exactly how we can measure up to the demands of this Chalupa Rule. Do your work and plan something fun at the end of your responsibilities. Don't let anyone take the fun away from you. You have earned it. It's yours.

If it's a crossword puzzle, then go for it. If it's reading your favorite magazine at your desk then *éntrale*. Pick your tasks and pick your pleasure. Do them in that order.

Chencha would be very proud. When you walk into a project at work and everyone is complaining about "So much work to do" and "Can't they see we're just human and only have one pair of hands?", you should just skip the whining and jump right into the work. Don't announce it. Don't brag about it. Just let *Chencha* help you get your work done.

Silently, to yourself, simply say, *A lo que te truje, Chencha*, and press on with the work. By the time others have finished fussing, your job is underway.

This Chalupa Rule can help you get all the other rules under your belt. All you have to do is go back and read the *prontito* part of a rule and put it into practice that very moment. That's what *Chencha* would do. You can do the same.

Ready. Set. Go.

A lo que te truje, Chencha. It's time to put all of these Chalupa Rules to work in your life.

A Lo Que Te Truje, Chencha

Do What You Came Here to Do

CHALUPA RULE TWENTY-FIVE

25

LA JAULA
The Cage

Turn Yourself Inside Out

Pónte al Revés

Prontito:

Many times we cloak our brightest talents and keep our potential under wraps. Let in some air. Shine in some light by letting people see more of what's inside.

A Lo Largo

Maintaining. Maintaining. Maintaining. We spend our entire lives making sure that our stuffings stay inside where they belong. We all walk around, our seams threatening to burst open and spill our deepest dreams and thoughts onto the street. The effort to keep ourselves together is exhausting.

Keep in mind an important Chalupa Rule, *Guarda tus frijolitos*. It is important to keep your precious, vital information and stores of self-esteem under safe lock and key inside of yourself. But there are other elements that make up who you are that really need to see the light of day. Do you have a sense of humor? Can you make people laugh? Are you a good storyteller? Can you hold an audience in the palm of your hand? Are there aspects to your personality that you keep inside for fear of ridicule or rejection? Then, my dear Chalupa, it's time to turn yourself inside out. *Pónte al revés.*

The Chalupa Rules have already told you how to "survive the laughter" and keep from burying your dreams when someone laughs or smiles at what you do. Now that you are able to do that, it's time to take the next step.

We have all had the experience of watching a performer, a standup comedian for example, forgetting their joke and actually saying to the audience, "Wow, I forgot what I was going to say." The usual reaction from the audience is not one of boos and hisses or calls for someone to chop off the comedian's head. What invariably follows is a wave of warm, reassuring laughter that tells the performer, "It's okay. We know you are human. Everyone makes mistakes."

Believe me, I know. My years as a standup comic have taught me to "call the situation." In standup comedy talk, that means actually admitting to the audience that your act is hitting a snag or perhaps even stinks altogether. If you stand there and forge ahead, oblivious to the uncomfortable silences and nervous coughs from a tense audience, you risk being a total flop. In every case that I have either seen or been a part of, "calling the situation" has saved the day.

It does involve "turning yourself inside out," revealing a bit of your inner workings so that people can see you are not some sort of *super-hombre* or *super-mujer* who always succeeds in leaping over the tallest buildings in one single *brinco*. No, you tell the world, "Hey, I made a mistake. I am human." That is part of turning yourself inside out.

You make a mistake at work? There's tension during a meeting? "Call the situation." Bring it up, make light of it, and press on.

Your children need to see that their parents are capable of admitting mistakes and learning from them. Don't hesitate to call the situation. Fight parental pride and let your kids in on a secret—parents make mistakes too.

This is also true in the world of broadcast journalism. During my early years as a news anchor, one stumble, one mispronunciation of a word and my television world came crashing down around me. The sweat poured out from under the thick canopy of hairspray that held my "anchor hair" together. The perspiration mixed with the pancake makeup and became a bright, pumpkin orange, making me look like a glowing, Mexican "Jack o'Anchor." Very nice. The tension not only colored my face, it tainted my performance as well. I wore the on-air mistake like a scar on my face for the entire world to see.

You soon learn that it's better to pause, say the word again correctly and move on. Yes, you make the mistake and move on. It's over. It's in the past. It can no longer haunt the present. You turned yourself inside out for the viewer. They caught a glimpse of an actual human making a real mistake. The world is not going to end. Don't linger over your mistakes like a rubber-necker fascinated with a bad accident.

Some weeks after the horrors of 9-11, the newscasts began to include other stories of the day: news, weather, and sports. However, we were all still traumatized by the experience of covering the World Trade Center disaster. Stumbles, hesitations, and mistakes were plentiful and for the most part, everyone reacted in an understanding manner.

One morning, while giving details of a sports story, I made a doozy of a mistake. Instead of reading the script as follows, "So-and-so is two hits shy of the record" I said, "So-and-so is two *shits* high of the record." Horrifying. I had actually said a "no-no" word on live television. Despite the laughter from the crew and the look of agony on my co-anchor's face, I tried to recover. I acknowledged my mistake with a sheepish smile and moved on to the next sports item.

I had definitely turned myself inside out and revealed that hey, everyone makes mistakes. My apparent ease in recovery had an interesting effect on some viewers. In one e-mail that we received, a viewer wrote to say that he and his wife were still aching from the tragedy of the Twin Towers. However, that morning, sitting on the edge of their beds and dreading another day, they heard my mistake and actually laughed for the very first time since the disaster. We were all in on the joke. It helped us all to heal.

Don't be afraid to turn yourself inside out, smile, and admit to a mistake.

We all get pimples. We all gain weight. We all age. Yet we spend a good part of our adult lives hiding the weight, covering up the zit, and finding ways to stay young. It is so liberating when you actually feel free enough to say to someone, "Hey, I have a zit," or perhaps "Wow, I've gained ten pounds. Must be all the tacos I've been eating." It helps people to relax around you and to know that you are being real with them. This is not to say that you put yourself down or turn words against yourself. You are simply saying, "Here are some of the seams that hold me together on the inside. I am revealing a refreshing glimpse of how I really think."

You have turned yourself inside out.

It's hard to do that sometimes when you stare at the cover

of magazines and see the glossy, super-human models portraying the fashion world's version of real people. Keep in mind that real people weigh more than ten pounds and actually have some meat on their bones.

Now here's the scoop. Real people rule the world. Take it from me. I have been on those high-fashion magazine shoots. The models are gorgeous, yes. But the clothes that seem painted on their bodies are cut and sewn to fit them specifically or are pinned in the back with giant clips to make it seem as if they fit perfectly. Imperfections the lights and makeup don't cover are smoothed over by post–photo session, computer wizardry. Those people are not turned inside out. Every flaw is sanded down, painted over, and hidden away. It is an illusion of perfection, a high-tech magic trick that sometimes fools us into thinking that theirs is the real world.

The most glaring example of photographic wizardry comes from an actual incident that occurred while doing a morning show. An author was on tour. The author will remain nameless. This person's photo was splashed across the front cover of their book, glamorous, gorgeous, and youthful. During the introduction to the interview, the camera dissolved from the book cover to the real person sitting in the studio. Let's just say the contrast was breathtaking. Real people rule the world.

The real world is me telling you that I am overweight. Years ago, I gave up the battle of staying ten pounds underweight for the cameras. I admitted to myself that I come from a family of *gorditos* and that is that.

Yes, I keep track of my health and scale back when the pounds threaten to spill way over my waistline like a giant blob of *masa para tortillas*. However, it is true that sometimes I order so much Chinese food that the delivery man brings it to my door with *eight pairs of chopsticks*. Special note: I live alone. One time I was compelled to shout into my *empty* apartment, "Hey guys, the food's here!" I don't care. I love Chinese food.

Yes, I love to eat. I eat when I am happy. I eat when I am depressed. I think about eating while I am eating. Admitting that is a relief and helps to turn myself inside out for you.

For years, I harbored this secret, burning desire. It was not for another person and not for a Krispy Kreme doughnut (although they do come in a close second). No, my dark secret was that I desperately wanted to try my hand at standup comedy. Years of being the class clown and decades of cracking last-minute jokes to break the tension of domestic turmoil sharpened my wit and helped me to "think like a standup." For years, I kept this dream safely locked away. I kept it out of the light and far from the eyes of the world. Finally, I could contain myself no longer and signed up for the The Standup Comedy Experience, a Manhattan workshop. The floodgates opened and years of one-liners and comebacks poured out. Still, I kept the classes a secret from my friends and family.

On the day I revealed my secret life, people were not surprised. They sensed my love of comedy already and wondered when I was going to try standup. I turned myself inside out only to discover that people sometimes sense things about you before you even know yourself.

Now I "own" the following truths about myself. I am a television morning show co-host, standup comic, playwright, and writer. I may stink at all of them but still I do them all to the best of my ability.

All of the above disciplines are now out in the open for the all the world to see and to judge. But at least now the most secret of professional desires are on the outside where they can actually do me some good.

In order to successfully *ponerte al revés*, you have to invoke the other Chalupa Rules that will help you along the way. We already talked about *Guarda tus frijolitos*. But make sure you keep this one in your back pocket as well, *No seas como pollo recién comprado*. Make sure you attack your passions like you are starving to death, someone puts a big plate of enchiladas in

front of you and you don't care who is looking. If you don't
believe me, then listen to this. That is how someone described
Lucille Ball's approach to her work, paraphrasing that she
performs like she's starving to death, someone put a big steak
in front of her and she doesn't care who is looking.

That, *mis amigos Chalupas*, is passion for your work.

Turning yourself inside out also involves finding new ways
to say the same old thing. I can easily say my New York apartment is full of Mexican decorations and is painted bright orange. It is quite another to say, "My apartment looks like a
mariachi threw up in it." You get the picture. Don't be afraid
to say exactly how you feel. Colorize your language, furnish it
with spicier, more interesting ways to say something.

Perhaps due to how I grew up, many times I find myself
freezing up. I lock up and become rigid, perhaps subconsciously trying to become invisible. This might be an involuntary response to the abuse and violence. But I know I am
trying my best to hide my flaws, to become the "best little
muchachito in the world" so that no one can hurt me. That is
such a crock of *frijoles*.

There is no perfect human walking this planet right now.
The more you try to hide what is inside of you, the more you
risk that it will fester and express itself in other, distorted
ways: heavy drinking, violence, or even depression.

One book I read a while back helped to illuminate this
grim possibility. In *The Gnostic Gospels* by Elaine Pagels, you
will find the following quote:

> *If you bring forth what is within, what you bring forth
> will save you. If you do not bring forth what is within you,
> what you do not bring forth will destroy you.*
>   —The Gnostic Gospel According to Thomas

Perhaps the tone is a bit strong, but you get the point. You
must let out what is inside and let it express itself. Your tal-

ents, your skills, your strong points—let them into the air and, as another Chalupa Rule says, "Let them shine!"

¡Dale chine! Letting your interior express itself not only has healing properties for you, it can also benefit others. Whenever I talk about my troubled growing-up years on television, I invariably get calls and e-mails from viewers who say they are glad someone is talking about issues that affect so many.

If you have a sense of humor, let it out! You can defuse many tense situations by injecting a note of humor. There are reasons people go to comedy clubs. They need a release from the everyday stresses of life. You can do the same in your own life if you try to find the "light side" of the world. *Busca la risa en la vida y la felicidad te encontrará.* Search for the laughter and happiness is sure to find you.

How do you feel about certain issues? Can you find the humorous spin on them and share them with the world? Plastic surgery is a good example. Someone asked me once if, being in the television business, I planned to go under the knife when the time arrived. I responded, "I don't care if I look like a Mexican Shar Pei when I get older. If they don't recognize me they'll just have to lift up the wrinkles, say 'Hi, it's Mario' and then drop them back down."

Perhaps it's because I didn't grow up with much. Perhaps it's because I have the fashion sense of a circus clown. No matter what the reason, I don't tend to follow the latest fashion trends of the day. If double-breasted suits are "out" you will still find them on me. I am not about to let a perfectly good piece of clothing go to waste. If I am wearing one black sock and a gray one, then so what? Nine times out of ten, no one notices.

Many times, I am the one who brings it up. I do take pride in myself and my clothes but simple, insignificant things I ignore and get on with my life. I have even shown my two different-colored socks on television.

It's a very liberating feeling to not be "rigid," glued tightly to the "got to do this" and "got to do thats" of *el mundo*.

Again, it's all about "being real," about letting some of your insides *para afuera*.

I dare you. Think about wearing mismatched socks to work tomorrow. You're thinking twice about it, right? Go ahead, it's not against the law. Do it. You will see it doesn't really matter and at the same time you let go of the sides of the swimming pool and splash around free of inhibitions for a while.

Turning yourself *al revés* is a process that reveals the seams and stitching that hold you together. The world can see more of how you are put together. People will feel more comfortable around you when you begin to feel more *cómodo* with yourself.

Share with coworkers a story you find funny and perhaps a little embarrassing about yourself when it is appropriate to do so in a conversation. Let go a little bit. Admit that you are scared about an upcoming job interview. Tell them how you got lost on your first day at work.

It's all about admitting things, owning up to the fact that you are human. The first time I performed standup comedy, I was so terrified it took me about ten minutes to lock my apartment door because my hands were shaking so hard.

I was so scared I went to the men's room just before going onstage and cut my finger on the paper towel dispenser. I spent my entire routine trying not to bleed on the first row of people. As we Tejanos say when something like that happens, "EEEE-embarrassed."

Admit to them. Own up to things. Share some of your insides. On the very first day of my very first job as a television news reporter I tried very hard to make a good impression. Too hard. Another reporter told a joke to a newsroom crowd. Everyone laughed. I laughed. I also passed gas at the same time and had to slink away in humiliation. "EEEE-embarrassed."

On my first trip to Europe I was fortunate enough to fly first-class. Out comes the camera and I take pictures of every single course of the luxury dinner that was served. In England, I poured lemon *and* milk into my cup of tea and then complained because the milk was sour. "EEEE-embarrassed."

I can't believe I just told you that. But I did.

Let's not forget the time I climbed onto a ledge in my SoHo loft and accidentally kicked the ladder away. I spent a few hours sitting up there in my underwear looking like some forlorn Mexican Humpty-Dumpty, my Chihuahua, Huitzi, staring up at me from the sofa with a look of disgust. "EEEE-embarrassed."

Then there was the time I tried to read a label without my glasses on. Minutes before going on the air, I sprayed my hair with window cleaner, slimy, greasy window cleaner. My hair looked like a shiny, black oil slick. I had to go on the air that way.

To make matters worse, my co-anchors decided to tell the world that Mario had "sprayed his hair with window cleaner." Nice. It turned out to be a fun and very "real" segment. But still, "EEEE-embarrassed."

Pónte al revés.

On the serious side of this Chalupa Rule, there are many times when I speak out on the air about my turbulent childhood. During a presentation of a "Hometown Story" segment on WCBS Television where I co-anchor a morning show, I clearly stated that my family was wracked with problems that include alcoholism, abuse, and domestic violence.

You can *guarda tus frijolitos* while at the same time letting down your guard just a little bit.

So, what are some ways that you can start turning yourself inside out? Here are some ideas. They go a long way toward helping the world to see your "insides."

One way is to talk about your experiences, share them with others. I was interviewed by *Marie Claire* magazine about their campaign to fight domestic violence. At the photo shoot, wearing a t-shirt emblazoned with the message that read, "It's

Time to Talk," I told my story of growing up in a troubled household. I am more than willing to turn myself inside out, even if it reaches out and helps only one person.

On the lighter side of *la vida*, taking a standup comedy class is a great way to find humorous bits and pieces of your life that you can share with others. Most major cities have these classes and they usually run from two to three-hundred dollars. In New York City, there is the Standup Comedy Experience, six to eight workshop sessions and guaranteed five minutes on stage at a comedy club.

Yes, it's nerve-wracking. Yes, you will lose sleep over actually performing onstage. And yes, you will learn things about yourself that can be presented in so many ways. Perhaps you are called upon to speak at a company or school function. These workshops can help you to develop your "persona," polishing your delivery and giving you confidence in getting up before a crowd. In addition, you will have an arsenal of jokes and one-liners that will set the crowd at ease. In my opinion, these classes are invaluable in opening you up to the possibility of letting people see what makes you tick.

If you want to expand your mind and take your communication skills to another level, then you take a workshop such as the one I am suggesting. It's like skydiving with words. You jump into an exhilarating process that reveals thoughts you have inside and allows you to "get things out" into the open.

Here is a sneak preview of some of the tricks you will learn in a standup comedy workshop. When you tell a story to a group of people, "Keep it moving." Don't stretch it out until you bore your audience. Get to the point, or the punch line, as quickly as possible. Enjoy your time at center stage and then move aside for someone else to have their moment. Always leave them wanting more.

Ahora por el ladio serio. There are great benefits to therapy. Getting counseling has opened doors to my interior that I never knew existed.

While you don't want to reveal everything about this to the entire world, it still is valuable as a way to peer into aspects of your personality and iron out issues that many times stretch way back into your childhood.

There is another important facet to this Chalupa Rule. Don't stop people when they begin to turn inside out for you. Many times, we put up "stop signs" and "red lights" when people begin to reveal details about themselves. Often, we are too concerned about our next turn to speak so we ignore the information others wish to share with us.

Listen with an open-minded attitude, fully aware that someone is sharing something special with you. While they speak, you will likely think to yourself, *ahora de veras te veo.* Now I truly see you.

To wrap up this Chalupa Rule, I want to say that being more open about myself and about how I grew up has been a tremendous growing experience. It's like I took a great big iron and smoothed out many of the wrinkles in the fabric of my life. It sounds corny but *es la verdad, amigos.*

When you are real, there is no need to be, as we Tejanos say, *papelero.* That means you are not some actor or actress playing *un papel,* or role, that others feel you should be playing in life. **You are yourself.**

Pónte al Revés

Turn Yourself Inside Out

26

EL TAMBOR
The Drum

There's a Long Distance Between Saying Something and Doing Something

Del Dicho al Hecho Hay Mucho Trecho

Prontito:

How far are you willing to travel in order to realize your dreams? It's very easy to state a goal or dream and it's quite another thing to actually turn it into reality. This *dicho* comes your way from the people who tried it over and over and learned it to be a valid truth of the world—your ancestors.

A Lo Largo

We all go around banging our very own public relations drum: "I am going to do this and I am going to do that." It is the simplest thing in the world, and the most tempting, to issue a press release or give out a sneak preview of the "coming events" of our lives. But, once we have done that, a long road stretches ahead of us.

The *camino* is unpaved, unmarked, and has no signs to point the way. It can be a very overwhelming feeling.

That's exactly how I felt when, living in a government home, I decided to try my hand at broadcast journalism. *¿Por dónde le voy a tirar?* "Which way will I go?" I thought. I had no roadmap to help me along the way.

But I had already told myself that this was the route for me to take. I am very careful about what I assign myself in life. Here is the reason why: If someone tells you to do something and you don't do it, that is a bad thing. In my opinion, if you tell yourself to do something and you don't, that's even worse. You have let yourself down. That's why, before you launch into a project, think long and hard about the effort it is going to take to make it come true.

Del dicho al hecho hay mucho trecho. Our Latino ancestors sure know what they are talking about. There can be a very long distance between your stated goal and the finalization of that dream. But, don't make a mistake that I often make and I am sure others make as well.

State your project, yes. But whatever you do, don't picture the journey to your goal as a straight line, devoid of problems and detours. If you do picture it this way, you are certainly going to face disappointment along the way. Whenever possible, I envision the journey to my goal as a sailing trip. I have never sailed a boat but I have watched people navigate their *barcos* along the water. The sailors take advantage of the winds that arise and seem to caress and nudge their boat in graceful curves on their way to their destination. I have yet to see a sailboat make it to its destination in one straight, unwavering line. The trip to your *sueños* is exactly like that, a winding path that, if you stick to your navigational plans, will eventually get you there. Remember, if you envision *una linea directa*, you will most probably be disappointed and abandon your project somewhere along the way. Be a sailor; be sensitive to the winds of opportunity, and fill your sails with possibility of a long, winding trip that will still transport you where you want to go.

While you are on your journey, be open to the reality that somewhere along the way, you may realize that this goal is not for you. Before you waste time agonizing over "What will people think if I abandon my goal?" remember one of my Chalupa Rules. You reserve the right to change your mind. It is as simple as that. You don't owe anyone much of an explanation. I have launched some projects that, in the end, were not for me.

Don't be afraid of what people will think if you change gears along the way. Remember, as long as you try something else you are still moving *adelante*/forward. I never want to be eighty years old, sitting in a rocking chair and wondering, "Hmm. Maybe I should have tried this or that." That is not for me. It should not be for you either.

Here are some things that I have tried in life. Some have worked. Others have not: Painting. Standup comedy. Playwright. Novelist. Television commercials. Theme park singer. Modeling. Delivery service dispatcher. Grocery store clerk. Electrical department salesman. At least I tried them all out. To be honest, the modeling experience was the most traumatic. My modeling career began and ended on the day that I fell off the runway. So much for my dreams of appearing in *GQ* magazine.

Yes, there is a very long journey between saying something and doing it. And yes, along the way you are going to try some things on and they are just not going to fit, like an article of clothing that is perhaps not the right size or color.

But, the *punto* of this Rule, my dear *Chalupa*, is that you are in the mix, doing things, finding out what's right for you in life.

On this long, hopefully very adventurous journey, try as hard as possible to do the things that you love. If your economic situation requires you to take a job that isn't exactly right for you right now, there is nothing wrong with pursuing your more pleasurable work pursuit on the side.

However, there is an important *advertencia* I want to share with you. While you explore other work possibilities, don't cheat on your main job. It is your career "spouse," so to speak. You must be faithful and pour your energies into a job well done. You can still go after your dream in your spare time. It is not easy, but it is possible. Do not cheat on your career *esposa o esposo.*

People sometimes wonder how I manage to do so many things. I work in television, perform standup comedy, write plays and books, while at the same time maintaining a rich, nurturing relationship with my family and friends. I have a mental picture that helps me. You may be too young to remember it but way back when, *en aquel entonces,* as we Latinos like to say, there was a performer on *The Ed Sullivan Show* who was a wizard at spinning plates. This guy would place a plate on a stick, give it a whirl, and then proceed to get other plates spinning just as fast on at least five other sticks. It was an amazing sight to behold. This gentleman was a genius at his craft. Never, but never did a plate fall, smashing into a million pieces on the ground. I feel there were two keys to his success. One, he never took his eyes off his spinning plates. His concentration level was laser-like, intense and unwavering. Also, he knew exactly how many plates to get spinning, not one more or one less than he could handle. Know your limit, get the "plates" (your interests) spinning and never let your eyes wander for a moment.

When you are starting your career there may appear what

look like shortcuts or easy-ins. Don't be fooled by them. They can lull you into a sense of comfort that may not really exist. Here's the reason why. I am fully aware that, once I stated my goal and began my journey, my ethnicity helped me along the way. I cannot prove it but I will bet you *un million de pesos* that at certain times in my career I have been hired because I am brown. Yes, that got me in the door, but that should not be enough. Being hired because you are Latino may get that brown foot in the door, but it's the rest of your body that is going to keep you there.

That *cuerpo* should be prepared with the best possible training and education to keep it employed because it's talented, not because it fits a certain hiring requirement. Now you are getting the picture; this Chalupa Rule carries quite a bit of weight.

You may state your goal. You may have some assistance at the beginning. But it is you and only you who can try on different interests and careers to see if they fit your life. It is indeed a long distance between saying something and then doing it.

Admit it. During that long, exhausting journey you will need a break, some time off to take a breather and reassess your life. It should not be one slogging march through muddy *problemas* and stressful *dolores de cabeza*. Pause for a moment, catch your breath, but at the same time keep one *ojo* on your goal.

These breaks in the long stretch between our stated goal and our final destination need not be expensive. My niece Alexandra and I always (especially when she was a child) would take advantage of what I like to call "free music." Free music is available just about everywhere these days.

1. Shopping malls
2. Department stores (Their music varies from department to department so you can practice all your different dancing styles while shopping)
3. Elevators
4. Record stores

Dancing with your children is a simple joy that they will always remember. One day, when they don't think that you are listening, you will undoubtedly overhear them tell a friend, "My mom/dad/uncle/aunt was so crazy, when I was a kid I remember dancing in the aisles at the grocery store."

Simple joys: Grocery stores on free sample day.

Car dealerships on days that they give free hot dogs and sodas. (Just don't forget to nicely—but firmly—say, "Just looking today, thanks.")

Take an inner vacation. Everyone always talks about the big, giant, expensive vacations that they take to points all around the world. Right in front of you, they unfurl their brochures and roll out their wagging tongues as they brag about the big trip they are about to take.

Yes, it's great to take one of those fancy trips. But what if money is short? What if you're too new at the job to take one of those fantastic trips? No problem. Do what I used to (and still) do. Take an "inner vacation." By that I mean pick a task or chore that you absolutely hate doing. Make sure the world won't end if you stop doing it though.

Then, go on vacation from it!

You don't have to tell anyone if you don't want to.

You can take an inner vacation from:

Ironing
Dusting
Re-organizing your files at work
Just about anything you want

Pick a length of time: a week, two weeks, three days. It's up to you. Then go on *vacaciónes*. It's a strange but wonderful feeling when you've given yourself permission to take time off from something you don't like to do. It's like you're a tea kettle and that "inner vacation" is a much-needed steam vent that will allow you to relax and unwind even though you're not boarding a plane or renting a car and buying sunscreen with an SPF of 1,000.

So let your big-mouthed friends have their big, blow-the-budget vacations. Relax and think to yourself, "Big deal, I am on an 'inner vacation' from cooking. It's all takeout for two weeks and I don't care who knows it."

Here is another point about this Chalupa Rule. Think about the times that you go on a long trip. You pack snacks, music, and reading material. You should do the same on this *viaje muy importante*. The most important item to pack is reading material.

By this I mean stock up on inspirational quotes and thoughts that catch your eye and make your heart beat faster when you think of your desired goal. Cut them out of newspapers and magazines and paste them on your wall.

Even if you don't read them every day, their message will be there when you need it. This is especially necessary when that dreaded emotion, fear, raises its ugly head and threatens to throw you off the path. If you feel a small measure of fear, some *miedo*, it is okay. It means you care, that you have passion invested into your pursuit. Read the quote I am about to offer you and let the words soak in to your soul. This comes from a newspaper clipping that is firmly pasted on my wall. I often refer to it when I feel that *miedo* creeping up my back. The words come from Roberto Benigni, the actor and director who created the incredible film *Life Is Beautiful*. The article talks about the fear he felt when he dreamed up the idea of placing his story in a concentration camp.

> "I was scared, but I was in love with the idea," Benigni says. "When we are in love, it is normal to be scared a little. It's healthy and very natural. But we must also be brave when we are in love."

Are you "in love" with the goal you have in mind? If you are, then that goes a very long way in getting you to reach that goal in life.

Like Roberto Benigni, we must be in love with our plans and ideas or we will never invest all the energy necessary to survive the very long journey that lies between saying something and making it happen.

There is more. In this journey to the finish line, opportunities pop up and many times we mysteriously avoid returning that phone call or put off the important meeting. I've been guilty of that many times. Just when it seems the golden opportunity lands in our laps, we shake it off as if it is a hot *tamal* that will only bring us more work and stress. This involves much more than my original Chalupa Rule, "The more you put it off, the more you put it on." We are avoiding something here. Let's ask the expert. Doctor Barbara Grande is a New York psychotherapist who has helped me to recover from the trauma of reporting on the World Trade Center disaster. Dr. Grande has also counseled me on personal issues with which I deal every day. That includes "skipping out" on *oportunidades* when they land in my path. Here is what she tells the Chalupa Rules:

Often opportunity is squandered because it is not perceived as the specific situation we believe we are searching for. Subtlety and possibility evade us as well as a belief in the serendipitous quality to every interaction. There is so much truth to fear of rejection and low self-esteem as reasons for procrastination. The negative "why me" attitude overwhelms rather than the positive "why not me" prevailing. It is very difficult to respond when feeling overwhelmed, and yet feeling overwhelmed is so much a part of our daily life. We must have a willingness to work with a level of anxiety and not project the "what-ifs." The challenge seems to be to stay in the moment. I think of three phrases: prioritize what is important, discipline to continue, and commitment to finish.

Even though the trip seems long, there is an interesting paradox that takes place. Thank goodness or this Chalupa

Rule would overwhelm anyone who reads it. At the beginning, when you are first starting out, it seems there are a million miles to travel until you land that job or finish that degree. There is a very big consolation. Every tiny step you take is one step away from your starting point. Every little *pasito* your feet make gets you a little closer to where you are going.

Just by being brave, as Mr. Benigni advises, that tiny step turns into a million miles away from where you first began.

Del Dicho al Hecho Hay Mucho Trecho

There's a Long Distance Between Saying Something and Doing Something

---

LA BANDERA
The Flag

Hold on to Your Flag

Deten la Bandera

Prontito:

Use your imagination to design a beautiful flag that represents all your hopes and dreams. Decorate it with your favorite symbols, colors, and objects. This is the banner of your identity. Never let it fall to the ground. This flag embodies who you are as a person. Hold your banner high through the toughest of times. Wave it in the air to show others that with your strength and your determination you will persevere.

A Lo Largo

I am sitting with my mother, Inez Alcalá Bósquez, in her new room at Mystic Park Care Center in San Antonio, Texas. I am crying as I write this because I know how this story is going to end. But this is for her, the woman who in so many ways gave birth to me, my dreams, and eventually the Chalupa Rules.

We make uncomfortable small talk as she lays uneasily in her new bed, in a place that is not her home. Caring for my ailing *mami* at our own house had become a sheer impossibility; she now needed the full-time, professional care that this excellent, state-of-the art facility could provide.

But the unsettling fact remains, she is not home. Her precious *casa*, even though only a few miles away, seems to belong to a distant universe, unreachable, forever out of her grasp. She is inconsolable and so is her family. Even this new "home" at the care center proves to be temporary. Within a month, Inez Alcalá Bósquez will begin her journey home.

For over twenty years, my mother battled a disease called scleroderma. This is a rare autoimmune disease that systematically attacks many parts of the body including the skin and internal organs. Inez Alcalá Bósquez, because of scleroderma, suffered a partial leg amputation, arteriosclerosis, osteoporosis, acute glaucoma, esophagitis, and a host of other ailments and conditions.

The most devastating of all is the final diagnosis of vascular dementia. It's described by some people as being, after Alzheimer's disease, the second most common type of dementia. All this happened to a woman known for her quick wit and colorful thoughts, all of that brilliance now condemned to a painfully slow fade-to-black.

Not fair. To a woman who raised six children under the stress of poverty and domestic violence. Not fair. To a woman who had a superior intellect and a heart of gold. Not fair to my mother. Not fair to any woman. Not fair to anyone at all.

And yet, despite all of the physical strikes against her, my mother rallied on, supporting her children and preparing them for the world of *Gringolandia*.

The disease never attacked and conquered her strength, her determination, or her sense of humor. They lived on.

Inez Alcalá Bósquez is a strong woman who raised her children while enduring that turbulent blizzard of negatives that always threatened to force her to cave in, to throw up her hands in despair and abandon her family. That never happened. She pressed on. She soldiered on. She persevered. Through it all, the struggle to put food on the table, the fight to feed and clothe her six children, and the efforts to recover from torrents of verbal abuse and physical attacks that included the plunging of a fork into her forearm during a particularly abusive confrontation, she kept going: for us.

In addition, this woman took on the responsibility of caring for her sister, Elia Alcalá, who suffered from rheumatoid arthritis. For over eight years, my mother cared for her sister until her own body simply wore out.

Let my mother's story stand for all the strong, beautiful Latina women who take their place beside their children and never stray from their chosen path in life. They are there for those who need them.

This brings me to the Chalupa Rule that both lifts me up and breaks my heart.

Deten la bandera. Hold on to your flag. Never let go of your banner.

It applies to so many circumstances.

Were you in pain and there was no money for a doctor so you relied on home remedies to see you through? Hold on to that flag.

Were there problems at school and some bullies were doing to their best to make you cry? *Deten la bandera.*

Of course, it is an imaginary flag, a make-believe banner of strength and determination that is blowing in the winds of your mind.

This *dicho* and now Chalupa Rule talks about your own personal *bandera,* the flag of your soul. When times are tough, when the situation seems almost impossible to bear, hold on to your flag. Hold it high and never let it waver.

There are, unfortunately, many occasions when our resources are low or nonexistent, when our last reserves of self-esteem are used up. These are the times for which this Chalupa Rule is intended. This Chalupa Rule gives you something to hold on to during trying times.

Let me hand to you your own personal flag of resolve.

Imagine a flag of your own design. Pick the colors to suit your tastes. Design the glorious emblem that will blaze from the center of its fluttering beauty. Make it as large as you want, as serious as you desire, or as outrageous as you dare.

Choose for your *bandera,* your flag, a sturdy pole made of the strongest, most durable wood. Attach it to your flag with fasteners made of the heaviest steel, impervious to any destructive force that might detach it from your beautiful flag.

Attach your *bandera* to this pole of survival and keep it handy, somewhere in a corner of your mind where it will always be within reach.

Don't hesitate to use it. When someone flings a discriminatory remark in your direction. When someone says that Latinos are not able to do a particular job. When a person with dark intentions tries to chip away at your hard-won self-esteem.

Reach inside your mind, pick up your flag, and hold it high in the air.

Through the trauma of discrimination. *Deten la bandera.*

Through waves of self-doubt. *Deten la bandera.*

Through shadows of depression. *Deten la bandera.*

The flag is yours. You made it. No one, but no one can ever take it away from you.

Never let it go. *Nunca.* It is one of your most precious possessions.

My mother, Inez Alcalá Bósquez, never wavered from holding her own flag high, a flag that also protected her family.

When we were too poor to buy food, had only three eggs for eight people and one egg fell to the floor and broke, *Deten la bandera.*

When in high school, as the only Latino to place in the top four in statewide speech contest, I'm told just before a newspaper photo is taken, "You can go home now." Through her tears, my mother's strength held me up with *Deten la bandera.*

When you lose your home through no fault of your own, the victims of a low-paying job and a strike at work, and you all have to sleep on the front porch of your aunt's house, *Deten la bandera.*

All of the above happened to my family and guess what? We are still here.

Through the long, arduous years of her illness, Inez Alcalá Bósquez held on to her flag and never let it go.

Toward the last years of her life, she always advised a close friend, Anita, that she should always *deten la bandera*, no matter what obstacles challenged her in life.

To my mother's credit, she carried on, flag waving high above her. But the terrible disease that ravaged her tiny body proved too much for her to survive. Scleroderma took our family's most precious heart, our mother, from us all too soon, at the age of sixty-nine.

During those awful times of intensive care and fading hope each and every family member had the chance to spend some final moments alone with Inez Alcalá Bósquez, born in Runge, Texas, and raised in another Texas town called Alice.

When my moment arrived, I felt powerless, completely devoid of any way to save my mother from this terrible disease. I wanted to give her something. I hadn't finished saying "Thank you." She attended each and every one of my high school speech contests, studied alongside me as I earned my college degree and she fought to complete her G.E.D., and she sent such strong waves of love and protection my way when I moved to New York that I could literally feel the love from thousands of miles away.

What could I give this woman who always fought for me, for my sisters, and now for her grandchildren?

"Nana, can you hear me?"

The soft whoosh of life-giving oxygen flowing into her mask was my only answer.

"Nana. I love you. Thank you. *Gracias. Gracias por todo.*

"Nana, you know the book I'm writing? It's for you. You made it happen with all of your love and your *dichos* that got us through so many tough times in life. You made it happen. It's your book. You're going to be *una estrella.* A star."

A pale cousin of her usually beaming smile peeks out from under the oxygen mask. She takes in every word of this last exchange between mother and son. *Hijo y madre,* trying to hold hands for an eternity.

"All of them, Nana. *Guarda tus frijolitos. Candil de la calle, oscuridad de la casa. Deten la bandera.* All them will live on. I love you, Nana. *Gracias. Gracias por todo.*"

One more kiss. Another embrace and I feel her frail, thin body bracing itself against the flagpole of her *bandera,* holding on for dear life. Even in these final moments, as she died, she showed us how to live.

In her last days, as she fought for her life in I.C.U., she received a visit from her good friend Anita, who whispered into my mother's ear as she struggled for every single breath, "*Deten la bandera.* Remember you always told me that. Now I am telling you, *Deten la bandera.*"

And so my mother did, until she took her last breath, at home under hospice care, surrounded by her children, grandchildren, and even beloved family pets.

You see, my mother's dying wish was to return home, to the place where she nurtured our bodies, our spirits, and our dreams. During the last stages of her illness, that trip home seemed impossible as the doctors and nurses tried everything that they could to save her life.

Finally, the doctors told us that there was nothing more they could do. We decided to take our mother into hospice care, to a center where she could die in peace surrounded by those she loved. And then it happened, as her family sat devastated and exhausted after days and nights in the waiting room, the hospice representative approached us to say that the hospice center was full, that there was no room for our mother. Our hearts stopped for a moment before she continued to say that instead, we could take our mother home and hospice care could be performed there.

My mother got her dying wish. Inez Alcalá Bósquez had somehow hung on through pain, morphine, and despair until her most fervent prayer became a reality. *Deten la bandera.*

I rode in the ambulance with my mother on that last journey. I saw her eyes drink in the stars that glittered overhead as they opened the doors of the ambulance and transported her into her cherished home.

I saw a flicker of recognition in those light brown eyes so filled with pain as she realized that she was indeed in her own bed once again in a room filled with "I love Nana" mementoes.

Even as oxygen tanks and other medical equipment imposed themselves into her precious space, she heard her very own television set humming warmly away in the background. It filled her room with a glow of familiarity and low-volume words of comfort from her favorite channel, Lifetime.

And it seemed as if a lifetime of love poured out of her eyes as I approached her bed, cradling her beloved poodle, Forrest, in my arms. Those eyes that had seen poverty, discrimination, and pain now gazed at her favorite pet. Those same eyes reflected the love, warmth, and memory of better times. Then, her eyes closed and resumed their chronicling of unfathomable, internal tidal waves of pain.

But she was home. The most cherished *casa.* A Latino's paradise where peace had finally reigned after years of heartrending physical confrontations, where love now ruled, and where death had absolutely no power over one woman's determination to *deten la bandera*.

She did so until she went home. Surrounded by *la familia*, she took her last breath and entered into well-deserved rest.

Until the last moment, she heard nothing but sounds of love and words of comfort.

For my mother, my family and I will never let go of our flag.

If a woman so wracked with pain can persevere, why can't we?

If years of abuse and decades of suffering fail to pry her banner from her hands, why can't we hold on to our dreams the same way?

If we have created such beautiful flags of identity, of power and resolve, why can't we hold on to them forever, through everything?

Even through the toughest of times, hold on to your dreams and never let them go.

Deten la Bandera

Hold on to Your Flag

CHAPTER TWENTY-EIGHT

LA CHALUPA
The Little Boat

Prontito:

The deck of playing cards also includes *La Chalupa* herself. She is resplendent in her traditional Mexican dress, and her colorful, off-the-shoulder peasant Aztec blouse frames a beautiful face. She rows a small boat, her *Chalupa*, as it is called in Spanish, with a look of pride on her face. Aboard the boat are lush fruits and flowers that are the ripe bounty of a successful harvest. Gather up all the Chalupa Rules and row your way to success.

A Lo Largo

This card represents all the cards put together. The little boat carries with it all the skills, proverbs, and advice onboard so that you can navigate life in the United States.

The Chalupa Rules fits into the modern landscape of life in the United States. As a fourth-generation Chicano, I decided it was necessary to open up the darkest corners of my life and formative experiences for inspection so that others can learn.

I have taken the clues from my own culture and upbringing to row my way through life in the United States. I have put all my cards on the table, open for inspection so that you can learn from my experiences. Take a good look at the Lady of *la Chalupa*. This beautiful woman is rowing her small boat that gives its name to this Mexican game of chance.

I see someone who is rowing her way through life with all the riches of a bountiful Latino harvest aboard. She has reaped the benefits of centuries of love, family ties, folklore, and hard-won lessons in life.

Like her, I am trying to load up my own *Chalupa*, my little rowboat, with a valuable bounty. The harvest that I share with you comes from the back of the Chalupa playing cards, old Spanish proverbs, and my own handcrafted rules of life.

They are saying to you, "It's a tough road to travel. I may have had some measure of success but my story is not over yet. The difference is that I am willing to admit that I am still struggling, still trying to find my way. So, let's walk together using these rules as lanterns to illuminate the path ahead."

They are honest, they are unvarnished, and they get to the heart/*corazón* of the matter.

I am the first full-time Chicano news anchor in New York City on English television and I still find myself holding back because I feel I am not worthy of speaking up and sharing my opinion. It has not been easy. But the way has been paved with encouragement from my family and with their homespun rules of life, sayings that are true and fundamental. The old proverbs are familiar to many Latinos. Their valuable insights and advice have been whispered into their ears for generations. The older relatives have always seen to that. The truths invested in them are direct and unfailingly honest.

No computer program is needed, no special dietary food has to be purchased, and no expensive electronic equipment has to be used.

Simply plug into this book and let the images of a simple game, the advice of generations, and the lessons of modern life take hold.

That is all the Chalupa Rules ask of you.

They have seen me through some very rough times. They continue to offer me support when my dreams are tested and when my resolve threatens to break down.

I started with nothing in this life and I may not have much right now, but what I do have I owe to these Chalupa Rules. I now share them with you, with other Latinos, and with anybody of any flavor who wouldn't mind having a simple roadmap to *Gringolandia.*

As I mention in the Chalupa Rule, *Deten la bandera,* many of these proverbs come my way via my mother, Inez Alcalá Bósquez. This book is for her. It salutes her towering strength and her determination to, at all costs, love and nurture her children. Unfortunately I couldn't name the book for her. The title *All About My Mother* was already taken. That's the name of my favorite movie by Spanish director Pedro Almodóvar.

A character named Agrado speaks these words and they never fail to inspire me, to lift me up, and keep me moving *adelante* with my dreams. The lines from the movie encompass everything that these Chalupa Rules share with you. Here they are:

Cuesta mucho ser auténtica . . . "It costs a lot to be authentic . . ."

. . . una es más auténtica cuando más se parece a lo que ha soñado de si misma. ". . . you are more authentic the more you resemble what you've dreamed you are."

Yes, there is a price to pay in order to become more authentic. You have to shed old behaviors and ways of thinking that hold you back.

At the same time, you need to hold on to your culture, your family, and your dreams. The price is the process of change, taking in new ideas, seeing if they fit and keeping the ones that work for you.

Sometimes all it takes is a different way of thinking, of reimagining the rules of the world in ways that make sense, ways that don't abandon what those who have come before us have learned. From that foundation, we build our own new rules that move us forward.

Read this line again: "You are more authentic the more you resemble what you've dreamed you are."

Make a copy. Paste it on your wall. Let your subconscious mind absorb it. What do you dream you are? How can the Chalupa Rules help you reach that dream? Only by living them will you ever know.

There is another step to these rules. They will inspire you to come up with your own *dichos,* your own handcrafted proverbs.

To that end, the last pages of this book are blank except for a simple blueprint similar to the structure of my Chalupa Rules. Perhaps you have mottos, sayings, proverbs that you are already using. Write them down in the structure of these rules and then share them with others.

You can also send them to askmario@chaluparules.com and I will add them to the growing "Guide to Gringolandia."

Yes, my little Chalupa Rules taco stand is open for business. The ingredients to a happy, successful life that includes family, friends, and a great future are sizzling on the griddle.

Here is a fresh tortilla. Let me wrap them up for you. The Chalupa Rules are best when ordered "To Go" so that you can learn on the run. Chase your *sueños.* Become your dream.

CHAPTER TWENTY-NINE

EL NOPAL
The Cactus

LA SANDÍA
The Watermelon

Bearing Fruit

Dondo Fruta

These images from the game of Mexican bingo lead off this chapter because it is time for the Chalupa Rules to show the results they are capable of producing.

The *nopal*, or cactus, produces a delicious fruit called a *tuna*. This juicy, shocking red delight delivers on its promise to refresh those who brave the thorns to reach its tasty interior. The *sandía* is already cut open. The watermelon's lush, velvety texture offers a devastating sweetness that is there, ready for anyone willing to negotiate the numerous, slippery black seeds that dot its sugary landscape. Are you willing to thread your way through the intricacies of your own life using the proverbs that our ancestors offer? Do you dare to peer into the "whys and why nots" that are at the center of our hesitations, fears, and anxieties?

Is there room in your busy life for new *dichos*, new sayings that are born from the struggles of daily life? If so, then this chapter is designed just for you.

It is one thing to display a list of rules and proverbs that help me. It is quite another to put the key into the ignition and turn the engine over. It hums and vibrates, pulsating with the energy of hope and possibility. This engine transported me through tremendous obstacles and sustained me as I dealt with problems that no child or young adult should ever undergo. This engine is still running. The mechanism is loaded with the proverbs and sayings that fuel my life. I know they will do the same for you. So, let's put the Chalupa Rules *en acción* and see where they will lead you.

I canvassed friends, relatives, and coworkers for questions that my Chalupa Rules can address. I want these rules to stretch their legs, warm up their muscles, and flex their power. These rules are designed to be applied to the toughest of situations and the most delicate of issues. The only request I make of anyone asking a question is to be "real," to spill their *frijoles* so that we all can learn.

Vámonos. Let's go. Time to dive into the ocean of Chalupa Rules that can help you to swim in the waters of *Gringolandia*.

‎—————

Dear Chalupa Rules,

I am a Hispanic married to an Anglo-American. How can I teach my kids to have pride in their Hispanic heritage?

‎—————

Querida Chalupa,

You are already taking the first step in helping your children connect with their *cultura*. You are reaching out to others and looking for ways to keep alive the centuries of tradition, culture, and values that are woven into the fabric of the Latino world.

My first duty is to tell you that the Chalupa Rules are firm believers in the concept of balance and fairness. Listen closely, *mi querida Chalupa*.

Your question is focused on "my kids' *Hispanic* heritage." That is a wonderful sentiment that brings the lovely *Sirena*, the Mermaid of the Chalupa, to tears. She loves to hear when Latinos express a desire to swim in the rich, bountiful waters of their culture. However, *La Sirena* wants you to know that you and your husband have a double responsibility where the issue of cultural heritage is concerned. Keep in mind that your *esposo*, your husband, also comes from a cultural background that your children carry within them as well. As you explore your heritage, he should do the same. Your children will benefit from the knowledge that comes from both your *culturas*. They will absorb these lessons knowing that both their parents care enough to present them with two rich *herencias*. *La Sirena*'s Chalupa Rule tells us to "Swim in our cultural waters." She is very comfortable navigating through the water and the air and she is just as beautiful in both elements.

That is the message you need to convey to your *hijos*, that the cultural heritages of both parents are equally important. *Querida Chalupa*, you do not divulge your spouse's cultural background, but let's say for instance that he is Irish. Then, there is nothing wrong with painting your kitchen a bright, bracing shade of tangerine (Latino-style) while including paintings and decorations that are elements of the Irish culture. Your entire family can swim in both waters. It is very important for your children to see that you are paying attention to all the cultures that make up who they are.

There is one very important question that both you and your husband need to ask yourselves. How well do you know your cultural history? The more you know, the more you can pass on to your children.

Oral history is a great way to begin. This does not involve going to the library and digging through stacks of history books. Although that is a great way to flesh out your *raíces*, your roots can be explored in an infinitely more personal way. You and your children can reach out to all your relatives and begin to construct a family tree, complete with the living, breathing stories that are alive with expression and color. Record them on audio tape. Videotape them for *el futuro*. Their stories are alive because they are told by people who either experienced them or were in contact with relatives who lived the pages of family history.

Many times, your children will be intrigued by the stories since they will, in many cases, carry the air and flavor of a mystery. Where was *Mamá Manchora* from originally and is it true that we have Jewish heritage?

Did *Papá Lolito*'s family really own five city blocks in downtown Guadalajara? From which tribe of Native Americans did your family really descend?

You can also go "high-tech" if you so desire, my dear

Chalupa. I did research on both sides of my own family and discovered our Native American roots along with more than just a strong hint of Sephardic Jewish heritage.

One day, while reading the *New York Times* I discovered an intriguing article that discussed the issue of DNA testing. This is where one of my favorite Chalupa Rules kicked in to action. *Sacude todas las ramas.* Shake all the branches. What more appropriate way to use this rule than to "shake the branches of my family tree"? I sent away for the DNA testing kit. When I received the package, I tore it open and immediately read the instructions. All I had to do was to swab the inside of my mouth with the cotton applicator and toss it into an envelope. Six weeks later, the results came in. There it was on paper, my exact DNA heritage. According to the test results, I am fifty-three percent Native American and forty-seven percent European.

I feel it's the high-tech way to say that I am a *mestizo*, a classic blend of the Native and European that make up most of the Mexican Americans in the world today.

The website that provides this information and testing can be reached at www.dnaprint.com. It is not an inexpensive test. It runs in the range of about $200 but can shed some light on your family's ethnic heritage.

You are already beginning to notice, *querida Chalupa*, that all of the above involves work, research, and family involvement.

If you truly dive into the cultural waters in which *La Sirena* swims, then you and your *familia* can build an activity that includes every single one of you. You are united in the bond of family history and pride.

In other words, you are no longer thrashing around in the muddy waters of "I don't know," and "Go ask your grandmother" when your children ask you questions that reach into the beautiful pasts from which both you and your *marido* emerge.

Like *La Sirena,* you will swim right up to them with answers. And if you don't have the answer you can work together to fill in the blanks.

If you combine this "family genealogy team" with an energetic effort to paint your life in the *colores de tu cultura,* then you are going a long way in instilling pride of cultural heritage in your *hijos.*

Buena suerte, querida Chalupa. La Sirena says, "Come on in. The cultural waters are fine." *Hasta pronto.*

Dear Chalupa Rules,

In my office my female coworkers are addressed as Miss Jones or Miss Smith and yet Hispanic females are addressed as Señoritas. I find this very offensive. How can I get my so-called "enlightened" male coworkers to address us appropriately?

Querida Chalupa,

This is a tricky work environment that you have found in *Gringolandia.* First, all Latinos know that addressing an unmarried woman as *Señorita* is perfectly acceptable. It is the proper form of address, unless the woman in question requests another form in which to be recognized. It is absolutely up to the woman involved. And that is exactly the case for you as well.

What I am sensing from your question is that you are hesitant to speak your mind. When this happens, remember one of my Chalupa Rules, *No te hagas chiquita.* Don't make yourself small.

Just like the other members of your office work force,

you have a right to be there. You also have the right to be addressed as you wish. Before speaking up however, monitor the situation for a couple of days.

Listen carefully. Are your coworkers, in perhaps a misguided attempt to make you feel "at home," trying to add some Latino flavor to the work environment? That could be the case.

But now, it's time to be real. Let's think for a moment like Latinos who have experienced both the subtle and overt signals of discrimination. Believe me, I have been there.

Those unfortunate experiences have created within us a special kind of "racism radar." It's a "sixth sense" that allows us to pick up on vibes that lean toward prejudice. In many situations, that "feeling" has been very much on target. There are many examples of prejudice that still exist.

One of my sisters has been aware of department store detectives "tailing her" while she shops while non-Latino customers are ignored. My cousin, who lives in a huge house in an affluent Houston neighborhood, still recalls the shock of her brush with bigotry. She was out watering her front lawn one day when a car pulled up. The window rolled down and a man poked out his head.

His question to my cousin who is, by the way, a lawyer and international banker? "Are you available to clean other people's houses?" She recovered in time to say, "No, I own this house." The car sped away. So, yes, we would be foolish and naïve to think the days of racism are over.

It sounds to the Chalupa Rules that, whether they know it or not, your co-workers are sowing the seeds of divisiveness in your workplace. It probably seems to you that every time they refer to you as a *señorita*, they somehow succeed in setting you apart from everyone else in your office. The seeds they plant grow hedges that separate you from the other women. The bottom line is that it bothers you and the problem needs to be addressed.

The question is, How? Keep in mind what I have told you, *No te hagas chiquita.* Don't make yourself small. Draw up your courage and your best office demeanor and settle the matter. If after your two days of observation and study you feel you have the right to speak up then do so without hesitation.

Don't over-explain. Don't wring your hands in self-deprecation and, most important of all, don't apologize. For example, don't say, "I'm sorry to bring this up and I don't want you to feel bad but . . ."

Instead, when someone addresses you in the manner that bothers you simply say with a smile, "Instead of *Señorita,* I want to be addressed like everyone else, as Miss or Ms. Sanchez. Thanks very much. Now, what did you want to talk about?"

Read the above once again, very closely. You did not apologize. You did not over-explain. You addressed the matter and moved on. Best of all, you did not make yourself small.

Usually a statement like that one, with the power of the Chalupa Rules "watching your back," will take care of the situation.

But we all know that every now and then someone pops up in the work force who doesn't know when to back off, when to listen to what someone is saying to them. In those cases, sometimes you will hear, "Please, you're being too sensitive about it."

Espera. Un momentito. Hold your horses. I have encountered that remark and I know exactly what to do about it. Just because you work in the nation's number one television market doesn't mean that you stop encountering discrimination.

Many years ago, at one place of employment, I made

a comment in reference to how minorities were treated. I heard the dreaded, "Oh you're just being too sensitive" line. Without skipping a beat, the answer popped into my mind.

My response, "Well, that's why they invented the word 'sensitive,' so that I can use it. So, here goes, 'I am sensitive to this issue. It bothers me. Let's address it and then move on to the responsibilities of our jobs.'"

Yes, every now and then, *querida Chalupa*, you have to rise to your full height, grab an issue by the *cuernos*, and make yourself heard. If, however, you take the matter by the horns and the problem persists, then quietly take the issue up the chain of command until it is taken care of to your satisfaction.

Hopefully it won't get to that point, but remember, Human Resources departments were put there for a reason. Take advantage of the services they provide. I promise, the next time I see you, the Chalupa Rules will gladly address you as "Ms. Chalupa." *Hasta pronto.*

Dear Chalupa Rules,

I'm a Hispanic Catholic female about to marry a Jewish man. His family expects me to convert to the Jewish faith without any regards for my feelings. It's not like my parents expect him to convert to Catholicism. What do I do?

Querida Chalupa,

Primeramente, felicidades, congratulations on your upcoming *boda!* I start with that greeting because you and your intended need to keep in mind that this is your wedding. Remember that as you deal with the situation of religion. It is your time as a couple to pledge your vows to each other, not to anyone else. Now I offer you a Chalupa Rule that may not at first appear to be appropriate to the question.

Siempre serás estudiante. **You are always going to be a student.**

¿Qué? What did you say? Isn't this question about marriage and religion? *Espera.* Wait a minute and you will see what I am talking about. You use the word "convert" twice. It has such a ring of finality, doesn't it? Convert. Permanent. No going back. I can only assume that in the process of getting to know each other both you and your intended, knowing you come from different faiths, made a conscientious effort to learn about the other's religion.

What? You didn't? You didn't think it was important? Those questions are mine of course but, judging from the urgency of your question, I can only assume that you in fact did not. It's not too late. Take classes in the Jewish faith. He should study Catholicism. You have stated that you intend to marry. You may convert someday to Judaism or he may one day convert to the Catholic faith.

Or you may both retain your original religious practice. But, dear Chalupa, no matter how it turns out, your children will have to grow up in a household where two strong and beautiful faiths are present. It is for them that you must make a concerted effort to learn more about the religion your husband-to-be brings to the marital table.

If you study Judaism and make a sincere effort to learn about it, you show your future parents-in-law that you care deeply about their faith and their values. Yes, make it clear that this process will not involve "conversion" but that it does involve learning and getting in touch with the most personal, spiritual aspect of their lives. That investment in their lives will go a long way toward showing them your level of commitment to the marriage. The same goes for your future *marido*.

Querida Chalupa, one phrase in your letter makes the Chalupa Rules worry just a little bit. You write that they want you to convert without "any regards to my feelings."

Have swords been crossed about this issue already? If so, now is the time to get it all straightened out.

Another step you can take toward family peace is to talk about the wedding ceremony itself. Check into the possibility of having a "double ceremony" where perhaps both a rabbi and priest can preside.

Be creative as one Chalupa Rule advises, *Sacude todas las ramas*. Shake all the branches of your life as you search for answers. This is an unusual comment but the Chalupa Rules believe in mentioning anything that might be of help.

Check your own family background. Did you know that many Latinos carry Jewish heritage as well? This makes us all realize just how closely related we all are at the end of the day.

As the Chalupa Rules mentioned at the beginning of the response to your question, this is *your* wedding and *your* marriage. It belongs to you and your husband with the rest of your family playing the role of "supporting cast." If you put in the energy to actually learn about their lives and faith you will also send out a strong message that this marriage is about patience, love, and understanding the spiritual values of your new *familia*.

Dear Chalupa Rules,

I'm engaged to be married, and my family is encouraging me to wait until I finish my undergraduate program. Should I?

Count your blessings, dear Chalupa. In the "good old days," many Latino families told their daughters what to do. Thankfully, those times of enforced futures are, for the most part, over.

However, you *do* show tremendous *respeto* for your family by taking their advice into consideration. The tone of your *pregunta* indicates you are contemplating a wedding before *graduación*, since you write that your family is "encouraging me to wait." What leads the Chalupa Rules to believe that there is a measure of impatience in your heart is that you do not mention how your "intended" feels. There is no mention of "us" or "we."

Dear Chalupa, you really need to have a "meeting with yourself" to explore the true reasons for your urgency. Why the impatience? As one of the age-old *dichos* from our ancestors advises, *El amor ardiente pronto se enfría.* Passionate love cools quickly.

Keep in mind the reasons for an engagement. It's a very serious "dress rehearsal" for marriage during which time you and your husband will have to learn the patience needed to land the right job, start a family, and buy the right house. An undergraduate program is challenging, time-consuming, and stressful. Adding the hectic preparations for marriage can only add to that pressure.

Perhaps you are not aware that you are really in "two" undergraduate programs. The other one you can call the "undergraduate" engagement program. When you finish that one, you move on to the "graduate program" of marriage.

Let's call it "Weddings 101." You take this class by buying a stack of wedding magazines and pretending as if your nuptials will take place in a few months. Make lists of wedding dress ideas, reception halls, bridesmaid dresses. The list is endless. Find someone who is in the middle of planning their wedding. Listen to them carefully. Go to a wedding dress shop and have a sincere *corazón-a-corazón* with the proprietor.

Pretty soon, the enormity of the undertaking will land on your shoulders.

But the Chalupa Rules cannot tell you what to do any more than your family is able to impose their will upon you. So you have to decide for yourself. *Recuerda*, you have already, by going into an engagement, promised to marry someone. This is the next step before you take vows. The time that leads up to your vows is a very important one. How much time elapses is entirely up to you and your husband-to-be.

If you feel you can handle it all, go for it. If not, then you owe it to yourself and to your intended to wait. Grab that diploma in your hands before someone slips a wedding ring on your finger. That way, you have tended your own garden before you move on to the larger pastures of wedded bliss. *¡Felicidades a los novios!*

Dear Chalupa Rules,

I have a good friend and it seems every time that we are about to buy something new, remodel our home, or go on a trip by the next week she's already done it. It's really bothering me. How do I go about, without hurting her feelings, telling her that she is copying everything I do?

I want to tell her, "You turn around and do everything I do." She does it all the time. We get a computer and they get a computer whether they need it or not. This throws the whole friendship into question. How do you go about this without hurting her feelings?

Mi Querida Chalupa,

It warms the *corazón* of the Chalupa Rules that you start your question with, "I have a good friend." That, *mi hijita*, is already a very good sign that your friendship is going to survive this cycle of "Keeping up with the Jimenezes." It is normal for any friendship to experience ups and downs as the years go by. One thing for sure, you need to address this problem now before it grows into bigger resentment and threatens to damage the entire relationship. There are definitely some tried-and-true Chalupa Rules that apply to your Latina "Lucy and Ethel" situation. It appears to me that you are playing the "Lucy" role and your "Ethel" *amiga* is simply following your lead in everything you do. When two people become "good friends" it is only natural that they develop similarities in taste and behavior.

Isn't that "compatibility" *la razón* you became friends in the first place? Even so, her "copycat" tendencies are getting on your nerves and that is good enough reason to settle the matter.

First and foremost, *querida Chalupita*, listen to this time-honored *dicho* that generations that came before us offer up to you. *Amigo y vino, el más antiguo.* "Old friends and old wine are the best." This proverb comes your way from a great book called, *Dictionary of Proverbs.* It lists many *dichos* that are as appropriate today as they were when our ancestors created them. In many cases, old friends *are* the best. You enjoy fun times and help each other through the turbulence of day-to-day life. We have to be careful not to throw all of that *en la basura* only because one facet of the friendship is "on the fritz." So, *a lo que te truje, Chencha;* let's fix the problem.

As "Lucy" to your friend's "Ethel," have you thought about the possibility that you are a role model for her?

Sometimes people are not enough self-starters to think up their own ideas or realize what they need in their lives. If you are *muy lista* and always planning and looking ahead, you may have inadvertently become the Latina version of a "personal planner" for your friend. At first, I am sure this seemed very flattering to your ego. It also must have felt great to be an influence on your friend's life.

But you are thinking, *basta ya.* Enough. You apparently don't want both your houses to look like cloned, carbon copies of each other. But if indeed your *amiga* simply looks up to you and values your advice and decisions then there is not much you can do other than try to cope with the situation.

In addition, you are talking some serious, major purchases here. This "copycat" syndrome has moved into the *mundo* of vacations, home improvements, and computers. As the low-riders in my old *barrio* used to say, that is definitely some serious *feria* being thrown around. That's some eyebrow-raising cash your friend is using to keep up with you. How long can that go on?

Only as long as you let it bother you, that is. Here are some Chalupa Rules you can use as a handle to get a grip on the situation.

Primero, perhaps you are your friend's Diana Rodríguez. Remember my Chalupa Rule that says, "Everyone needs a Diana Rodríguez"? In a nutshell, you may be acting as the impetus that gets your friend onto the "dance floor" of life, giving her the ideas and energy to buy what her family needs. It may not be "copycat" at all but more a case of role-model/hero worship. There are worse things in friendship than that, *mi Chalupa.* It feels good to be liked and admired. Are you uncomfortable with that? Perhaps you should reassess your feelings of self-esteem and allow someone to follow your lead in life.

You also have to realize that these major purchases are big decisions that your friend's family has to make.

It is not just her whipping out that *tarjeta de crédito* and making trips, computers, and who-knows-what-else materialize into her *familia*'s life.

Many, many times, *le hacemos ruedas a los problemas.* We run circles around our problems, going around and around until we make ourselves dizzy with all the possibilities. In this muddle, resentment builds and we create scenarios that just aren't the case. Be real with yourself, does she really purchase everything you also buy?

If indeed you are good friends and there is a level of humor involved in your interactions, then there is nothing wrong with injecting a lighthearted comment now and then as you and your *amiga* enjoy *una taza de café con leche.* "*Ay comadre*, it looks like every time I say I'm gonna buy something you go out and get it before I do. Is this a race or something?" Start with humor and see what response you get.

There is another Chalupa Rule that you can use. *Guarda tus frijolitos.* Always keep a little pile of beans to yourself. It is not necessary to always divulge your future plans, purchases, and vacations. Sometimes in our excitement we spill all of our *frijoles* for the entire world to see. *Guarda tus frijolitos.* Keep a reserve of information to yourself and perhaps it won't be so easy for your friend to rush out and beat you to the punch.

Your situation calls for another dose of the Chalupa Rules. This one calls for discipline on your part. *En el camino de la vida, no mires para los lados.* I had to create this rule for myself very early in life.

Growing up poor and disadvantaged, we were surrounded by those who had more. Perhaps they owned a new car or had brand-new clothes to wear. We struggled along with ancient, used cars that always broke down. We wore secondhand clothes that should have been thrown in the rag heap months before. We had no choice. However, as a child, I was always tempted to look into the neighbors' backyards and inside their houses and marvel at the wonders that having more money could perform in someone's life. But every time I looked to the side, I slowed myself down. This, dear Chalupa, is what I feel you are doing to yourself. You are so concerned with the actions of your *querida amiga* that you are taking the focus away from the important details of your life. Don't look to the sides as you proceed in life; concentrate on the important matters at hand.

Their money, credit cards, or savings are making the competitive purchases. To put it *fuertemente*, very bluntly, we are talking about their funds so there is not much you can do about that. Just what is really behind the "*barrio* buying spree" your *comadre* feels compelled to undertake? Your good friend may suffer from low self-esteem and perhaps some sort of shopping compulsion. She may see your purchases as a "green light" to whip out the cash. Or, she may view your newly acquired goods as a reminder that her life is, in some way, inadequate and lacking.

That's where your job as a "good friend" kicks in. Compliment your *mejor amiga* on what she already possesses.

Reassure her that her family and her possessions are wonderful parts of her life, to be admired. She may be looking for reassurance. That's something you can give her that no credit card can buy.

If you have a spirit of community involvement then here is a golden opportunity to get your friend involved in your pet charities as well. You are already pretty good at announcing all your future plans and purchases anyway. So, simply add to that list your plans to volunteer at your favorite charity. Or, talk about your donations to the local shelters. If your "good friend" is truly a good one, she will do the same and you will be helping *la co-munidad* at the same time. If she's going to be a "copy-cat," she might as well do it for a good cause.

Dear Chalupa Rules,

My daughter wants to have a "debut." No one in my family has ever had one before. It is against our faith. She is going to be fourteen and wants to have what other girls are having. Mom and Dad are not happy because there is going to be a dance, which is also against our faith. What do I do?

Queridos Padres Chalupas,

Bienvenidos to the world of teenagers. *Primero,* I want to explain to non-Latinos that a "debut" or *Quinceañera* is a fifteen-year-old girl's "coming out party."

This official presentation to society is very common among most Latino communities and for many, it is a highlight of a young girl's social life.

The *Quinceañera* features a Catholic Mass, a dinner, and usually a dance. That is where the *problemas* begin for your family, I fear. The entire idea of a "debut" is against your religious beliefs. Yet, you have *una hija* who is surrounded by friends who are either busy with their own celebrations or making preparations to appear in a friend's debut. You must understand that is a tremendous amount of pressure for a young person to experience in such a formative period of their lives.

However, it is also important to take into consideration the religious beliefs your family holds dear to their *corazones.* It's easy to see from your *pregunta* that these are long-held, steadfast beliefs that span at least two *generaciones*. The Chalupa Rules can see that because you state that no one in your family has ever had a debut.

And now here you are, faced with a major family and religious dilemma. How do you nurture and support your daughter, who is making the transition into young adulthood, while at the same time hold fast to your faith?

There is an answer here but you can only find it by using one of the Chalupa Rules. *Sacude todas las ramas.* Shake all the branches. The objective here is to have a celebration with which both you and your daughter can be comfortable.

The Chalupa Rules imagines that you have raised your *hija* under the roof of your faith and that she is well-acquainted with its rules and regulations. In addition, if you have done your job as *padres* and spiritual advisors, she is in touch with the requirements that your church has set down for its followers.

Now it is time for you to get to work. By shaking all the branches, the Chalupa Rule means that you must take the time and make the effort to explore all the possible ways to give your daughter a celebration that she will enjoy while at the same time staying within the boundaries of your church. It is important that you immediately schedule a series of meetings with your religious leaders to find out what is allowed and what is forbidden. Your daughter will see that you are making a concerted effort on her part to give her a special birthday observance. That will mean a lot to her. She will see that her parents, instead of crossing their arms across their chests and saying **NO**, are making every effort on her part.

Remember another Chalupa Rule that will keep the entire process from feeling like an overwhelming ordeal. *No tiene ciencia.* There is no science to it. That means you take the exploration on a step-by-step basis.

Make a phone call. Schedule a meeting. Read literature about your faith that explains its rules in detail. *Paso a paso*, the path will become clear.

From the vantage point of the Chalupa Rules, the scenario in your *casa* looks like this: You and your spouse are standing on one side of the living room and your daughter is on the other, a line drawn clearly down the middle.

Yes, a debut. No, a debut. But *queridos padres Chalupa*, did you ever consider a middle ground? *Un poquito tú, otro poquito yo.* You give a little. I give a little.

What are the possibilities of a special religious observance followed by a nice brunch or dinner? In all cases, make the religious portion of the celebration the most important part and you will prove to your religious elders that you have a sincere interest in following the tenets of your faith.

Make a list of the all the possible ways to have a *Quinceañera* without actually calling it a *Quinceañera*. This is not merely a case of "playing with words." You are structuring a rite of passage that will satisfy all the parties involved, especially your daughter.

Is it possible to have the religious observance and dinner and *then* a small dance with a D.J. at another location? Attendance at this part of the celebration would be strictly optional and not at all a part of the main event.

The bottom line is this. You have a strong, beautiful foundation in religious faith, one that the Chalupa Rules is certain you have also instilled in your *hija*. You do not have to compromise that in order to give your daughter an unforgettable fifteenth birthday that, even though it carries the weight of religious and social significance, does not have to fall under the category of *Quinceañera*. The Chalupa Rules assures you that later in life your daughter will remember that you cared enough to remember her special day while *al mismo tiempo* holding your religious beliefs close to your heart. *Buena suerte y feliz cumpleaños* to your *linda y joven Chalupita.*

Dear Chalupa Rules,

How do I get it the point across to my dad that he considers me the black sheep of the family? He treats me differently from my brothers and sisters. If I go to his house to help him he tells me "*Tú no sabes nada*, you are doing it all wrong." Then, my brother does the same thing and he doesn't say anything. It's been going on all my life. I have always been treated differently. How do I deal with that?

Querido Señor Chalupa,

The Chalupa Rules feel your pain. We have all experienced the sting of parental rejection in one form or another. In your case, you feel that it has been a lifetime of *mal tratamiento* and for that we are truly sorry. Please read this Chalupa Rule very carefully, *con mucho cuidado.*

No hay mal que por bien no venga. Our ancestors handed down this proverb for very good reason. In their long lives and their experiences, they realized that even from the darkest moments in our lives, there is something we can learn.

Querido Chalupa, you apparently have endured many years of being treated like the black sheep of the family. It is time for that to end. You have your *manos* on the steering wheel of your life. Guide it to more peaceful territory. The Chalupa Rules want to prepare you though. Before you get to smoothly paved roadway you will encounter big potholes and ditches that will threaten to stop you in your tracks. No matter what happens, keep driving onward. You will reach your goal.

Yes, you have experienced bad things, the feeling of rejection from your father. But despite that, you appear to be a dutiful son, going to your parents' house to help with chores. This proves that you survived the turmoil to still be a contributor to your family's well-being. Too few people in this *mundo* possess that capability to persevere.

What the Chalupa Rules are telling you is to take stock of all the wonderful, positive things that you are as a *persona*. No one, not even a parent, can take those qualities away from you. They are yours, *para siempre*.

Now it is time for the Chalupa Rules to roll up their sleeves and get very serious with you for a moment. My background as a journalist for over two decades has taught me extremely valuable lessons in human nature. Here goes: There are always two sides to every story, and the truth can always be found somewhere in the middle.

Escúchame. Listen to me. Dig into your past. Take advantage of another Chalupa Rule and actually have a "Meeting with yourself."

Did anything happen between you and your father that could be perceived as a stumbling block to your relationship? An indiscretion of youth? A violation of family rules? Think carefully and be brutally honest with yourself. This may be the sticking point in creating a positive, loving relationship with your *padre*.

If you do come up with something, take it to your father. Discuss it openly with him and tell him that you are aware of the tension between you. If there is nothing in your past that is blocking your "father connection," then you still have to meet with him and talk matters over.

Yes, you are his son but you are also an adult who

should make every effort to shore up his reserve of self-esteem. Tell your father exactly how you feel. Express to him that you feel "like the black sheep of the family." However, when you do that, make sure you cite concrete examples from your life. Keep them short and unadorned, devoid of emotional detail that will further cloud the issue.

One of the basic properties of the Chalupa Rules is that you should take comfort in whatever proverbs, sayings, and mottos you encounter in life. The Chalupa Rules cannot remember if Dear Abby or Ann Landers said the following but since they were sisters we are sure they wouldn't mind being quoted together. Paraphrased, the advice to one reader was, people will only get away with what you let them get away with. The Chalupa Rules feels that includes parents as well.

If you couch your thoughts in words that say, "Papi, I love you. I adore and respect you and Mami more than anything else in the world but the way you treat me hurts my feelings," then your father can't help but hear the caring and concern in your voice.

Cuidado, here is where the turbulence can begin.

No one can predict how a parent will react when a child confronts them with their innermost feelings in one fell swoop. For that reason, the Chalupa Rules advises you to *consultar con tu almohada* and decide exactly when and where to face your father. In the time leading up to that, make sure you express all your loving feelings to him and your mother, lay the foundation for the words you will eventually say. That way, they will not come like *un relámpago,* a lightning bolt from the sky. It is always better to deal with concrete issues than abstract "accusations." You may have to wait until your father actually says, "You don't know anything." Then ask him what he means.

Wait until your brother does something the exact same way you did without experiencing your father's recriminations. Then, ask him why there is a difference in treatment. It is more difficult to avoid the "hard evidence" of an actual occurrence rather than reach back into the fuzzy, distant past to dig out something that happened *en el pasado*.

No matter what the final outcome, you must hold tight to the values and qualities that you possess and like the Chalupa Rules have already told you once before, no one—not even a parent—can take that away from you.

CHAPTER THIRTY

30

LA CORONA
The Crown

Something Extra
El Pilón

We Latinos love the concept of *El Pilón*. It's the "something extra" that shopkeepers toss into your bag just before you head out the door. Think of a Spanish-flavored baker's dozen. I want to be like those old-time store merchants that many of us remember fondly.

Let me top off your shopping bag full of Chalupa Rules with a collection of traditional and handmade rules. *La Corona* from the game of Chalupa is the image because the "crowning glory" of the Latino heart and mind is the ability to stay in touch with our *cultura* as we navigate the waters of *Los Estados Unidos.*

These Rules are flexible. They are not fixed in concrete and frozen in time. As Latinos, we can all come up with brand-new Chalupa Rules that work in different challenging situations as we make our way through *Gringolandia.*

Mis queridos Chalupas, here is your *pilón* for being so kind as to buy this book and take it into your *corazón.*

On borrowed things is where sorrow falls.

En lo ajeno cae la desgracia.

This old proverb warns to take extra care when handling an item you have borrowed. It seems to be an unwritten "rule of the universe" that the item someone lends you is the first thing that breaks or is lost. You must double your efforts to use whatever is borrowed with extreme care and then return it exactly as it was entrusted to you. Pretend the item really belongs to you, that you paid the money to purchase it.

I borrowed a car from a friend one time and on the way to a huge event in Washington, D.C., I was involved in a minor fender-bender.

Not only was I two hours late for the event, I almost left her without a thing to wear because in the back seat of her car was the expensive, designer dress she planned to wear at the gala that night. Thank goodness she had a last-minute, back-up outfit. This was a tough lesson in "on borrowed things is where sorrow falls." *Mucho cuidado* when you borrow something, okay? Treat it as if it is part of the crown jewels. Later, people will be more than happy to lend you something once again. Unless, of course, they have a designer dress in the backseat.

Don't think backward.

No pienses al revés.

This Chalupa Rule goes hand-in-hand with *El diablo nunca duerme.* The devil never sleeps. We are constantly tempted to think backward. That means we take an action first and think of the consequences only later. These are consequences you knew existed in the first place. Examples: When we use phrases such as "I couldn't help it," "Something just came over me," or "It was bigger than the both of us," we allow ourselves excuses for ignoring the consequences that we knew existed before taking any action at all. You absolve yourself of any blame for mistakes in your life, something bigger than you (the devil) has "made you do it."

The point of this Chalupa Rule is that you *can* help it. Something didn't just come over you, you *wanted* to do it. Take action for your responsibilities. The devil comes in the guise of bad choices in life, an energy that compels you to think backward. You may know something is wrong but you do it anyway and then wash your hands of blame. That way, you get the pleasure of doing whatever it was you wanted to do, as if you didn't know the consequences in the first place.

The devil never sleeps. He is always trying to get you to rationalize your behavior. Think of the words you are using. Take them apart and you will find the place where the devil never sleeps.

The next time you do something and say "I couldn't help it." Stop. *Piensa.* Think about it and be true to yourself. Realize you could have "helped it" but decided not to do so. It was a choice you made.

Your presence does make a difference.

Tu presencia, hace la diferencia.

Sometimes we think that our presence is insignificant, that our contributions to the world are small and inconsequential. However, every little step we take toward improving ourselves and our *familias* can be felt way down the "timeline." I still remember the kindnesses, the words of comfort, and the doses of encouragement given to me years ago. The words may have seemed small and of no great importance to the person who said them but they still mean something to me. Years ago, while working in radio, I was worried about getting that next job and moving on. Someone told me, "Trust your talent. Whatever you have learned in life is not going to be erased. It will not go away." Too often we feel that what we have learned has little or no value to the rest of the world. We feel that one day we are going to wake up and our skills will have vanished into thin air. That is not going to happen.

But do use those skills to make a difference at school or in the workplace. Make your presence known.

When my contract at a television station ran out and I decided to move to another place of work, one of the first things management did was to take my picture down from the wall where the main anchors were featured. That is normal procedure but it still feels strange to see your photograph come down. Hey, whether we admit it or not, we all have egos. But that picture held particular significance for me. I was among the first Latino news anchors at that station and the first Mexican American anchor it had ever known. On my last day, I walked past the wall and noticed that where my picture was there remained only a tiny hole where the nail had been.

It may sound crazy but I called a producer friend over, pointed to the wall and said, "See that hole in the wall? That little hole? That's all that is left of where my picture used to hang. But I want to tell you something. Even though that tiny little hole seems like nothing, it means a lot to me. It means I was there. I was present." *Tu presencia hace la diferencia.* Your presence makes a difference.

An apology is simply a wet bandage.

Una disculpa es solo un vendaje mojado.

I had to learn this Chalupa Rule the hard way. So many times in my life, someone took advantage of me, was cruel in some way, shape, or form, or simply went out of their way to hurt my feelings. Then comes the apology. The "I'm sorry." Whenever someone does something intentionally hurtful to me, I try to ignore it but if they come up and apologize I have a unique way of dealing with the matter.

Due to the fact that I have experienced physical and mental abuse in my life, I know many times that apologies are simply "wet bandages." They don't stick for very long.

You may hear the "I'm sorry" but in fact you are fully aware that this person is capable of repeating their act. That is usually what happens.

I have learned that when some people offer up an apology they are, in fact, subconsciously asking for permission to do it again. That is something that my hard-won self-esteem will not allow to happen.

I do give people plenty of credit for apologizing but, if I sense that repetition is just around the corner I respond in the following manner, "Thank you. Yes, I hear your apology and recognize it. However, accepting your apology does not mean that I give you permission to do that to me again." Then, after that takes place, it is a "clean slate" with that person, a fresh start. Now they know that self-esteem is something that people protect, something they value, and they are expected to do the same.

If you are at all like me, what self-esteem I now possess is hard-won and I am not about to let it go.

Good grades will never disappear.

Los buenos grados nunca se van a acabar.

That is the wonderful thing about working hard to bring home a healthy report card full of good grades. Unlike allowance money that disappears almost as soon as you get it, good grades are here to stay. You can never spend them until they run out and disappear from your report card. Be assured the "A" or "B" you earned in the first grade is still there.

If you don't believe me, go to the box where the card is stored and take a look. Those good grades are recorded forever. Even though they are tucked away in the dark, collecting dust, they still contributed to the other great marks and achievements you have received in life. You can always spend a dollar, watch it vanish into the cash register never to be seen again. You cannot spend a good grade that way. You can use it over and over and it will never run out.

As young children who grew up in a disadvantaged home, my sisters and I were strangers to the finer things in life. But I will never forget what one wonderful physician told me during a routine, physical check-up. Doctor Karl Hempel, knowing our financial situation, told my family that an "A" or a "B" is like money in the bank, money that will never run out. Those good grades, he said, will translate into scholarship money for the future. Doctor Karl Hempel is right. Tell your *hijos y hijas, los grados buenos nunca se van a acabar.*

Once a farm dog has eaten chicken eggs he'll keep doing it no matter how you discipline him.

Un perro que come huevo aunque le quemes el osico

Boy, is this ever a "countrified" Chalupa Rule. It goes back to the days of backyard chicken coops and farmhouse dogs. Old relatives used to say that once a dog got a taste of hen-house eggs there was no way you would ever get him off the "habit." This proverb means that once someone gets of taste of being bad or "naughty," it's very hard to change their ways. Once a cheater?

Tell me who you're with and I will tell you who you are.

Dime con quien andas y te digo quien eres.

This is the perceptive, intuitive Latino version of "birds of a feather." This old *dicho* states that once I know with whom you keep company, I can tell more or less what kind of person you are.

You don't have candles at this funeral.

Tú no tienes velas en este entierro.

Wow. What a darkly poetic way to say, "None of your business." But that is exactly what this old *dicho* means. It is telling you, or someone who offers opinions into matters that do not concern them, that they have no business doing so. Symbolically speaking, you have lit no candles to the "person" who has passed on. You do not have any history or emotion invested in their death so for that reason you really have no business being there.

This means you aren't directly involved in the subject matter being discussed. The proverb is a sign posted on fence. The bold, funereal black letters clearly say, "Private Property. No trespassers." Do what the sign and the *dicho* command, keep out.

There is no bad from which good doesn't come.

No hay mal que por bien no venga.

This proverb is often used when misfortune falls upon you. It tells you to consider the possibility that you can always learn something when something bad happens. It advises you to "take stock of the situation" and try to pull out a valuable lesson.

A barking dog doesn't bite.

Perro que ladra no muerde.

This Chalupa Rule wants to reassure you that rarely does a "loudmouth" deliver on their threats and bluster. It is similar to the traditional English proverb about a dog being "all bark and no bite."

God does not hear he who does not speak.

Al que no habla, Dios no lo oye.

This proverb advises you to speak up. This piece of advice is especially valuable in loud Latino families where everyone talks at the top of their lungs. You want something to drink? Speak up. You want something to eat? *Speak up!*

Passionate love soon cools down.

El amor ardiente pronto se enfría.

There is nothing more exciting than ardent, reciprocated love. It sets the heart afire and inspires poetry or very bad rap lyrics. But this ancient proverb quickly throws cold water on *corazones* that are beating too fast for their own good. It advises romance with a slower speed, an old-fashioned courtship. With these "hearts and flowers" in mind, I want to share with you, my Chalupa friends, a true gem of romance. Many years ago, my late grandmother, Toribia Cortinas-Bósquez told me about the courtship rituals of years gone by.

They included a charming process in which the sweethearts traded poetry verses back and forth. One of those short poems dealt with the issue of slow romance. Here it is in Spanish:

> *Cerca de mi casa tengo una parra floreando*
> *¿Cómo quieres que te olvide si apenas te ando enredando?*

It translates as follows:

> *Next to my house I have a vine growing.*
> *How can I forget you if only now I'm entwining you?*

It sounds much better in Spanish but you get the picture.

Nobody sells their best steer because he's "so good."

Nadie vende su macho por bueno.

This traditional proverb comes straight from the ranch. It's a Latino version of "buyer beware." The saying warns you that no one is going to sell their prized animal because he is so great. It seems they may be trying to unload their "worst" livestock/merchandise first. Think of all the times a high-pressure salesperson tried to pawn off a big-ticket item and you later discover it's of low quality. Perhaps someone pushes you to buy their old car because "It runs great and never breaks down." Yeah, right. We have all been there. Enough said. So, if someone tries to get you to buy something "because it's so great," be careful. If it's so wonderful, why are they trying so hard to get rid of it? Think *dos veces*. They may be trying to unload their bum steer.

Bread can soften the sorrow.

Las penas con pan son menos.

This proverb has been around for generations. If someone is having problems, experiences a death in the family, or is in general just moping around the house, then usually an older relative will try to feed them.

As a matter of fact, in Latino households, food is seen as a remedy for many emotional ills. Sometimes you want to fake it and say you're sad so that someone will immediately shove some delicious Mexican, Puerto Rican, or Dominican food in your mouth.

The month of February is crazy but March is even crazier.

Febrero loco y Marzo otro poco.

This proverb that deals with unpredictable winter weather and the instability of an incoming spring has a very short shelf life. You can really only use it during the two months to which it refers. However, feel free to use it when talking about two friends and how one might be "wilder" or "more fun" than the other.

This child is not a Holy Water font, where everyone has a hand in his discipline.

No es pila de agua bendita, para que todos le vayan a la mano.

This saying refers to the font of Holy Water that can be found at the entrance to most Catholic churches. Everyone entering the church would dip in their hand in as they entered the sanctuary. This phrase dictates that not everyone's hand should be used in disciplining a child.

This *dicho* clearly states that the raising of a child is strictly the parents' territory. There were very strict rules regarding discipline in our family. No one other than the child's parents could administer reprimands or punishment. God forbid if someone other than the parent spanked the child. All-out war could break out.

Don't take off your life jacket before it's time.

No te quites el salvavidas antes de tiempo.

This Chalupa Rule popped into my head at the strangest of times. Many years ago, my family was enjoying an outing at Medina Lake which is just outside of San Antonio, Texas. We barbecued and splashed around in the water, having a great time. One of my sisters, who will remain nameless, wasn't the best of swimmers. For that reason, we put a life jacket on her to make sure she didn't drown in the cold, dark lake waters. After bobbing up and down for a while, this sister decided that the life jacket was getting in the way of her fun times. She asked me to remove the flotation device so that she could maneuver more freely. I knew better. The life jacket had created a false sense of security, creating only an "illusion" that she was a capable swimmer. But she insisted and being the good yet devious brother that I can be, I swam over and unfastened the life preserver. Immediately, this Hispanic "Esther Williams" dropped like a rock. I pulled her from the depths and, as she sputtered out the lake water, I managed to squeeze in a lecture about rushing things and trying to do something before it's time.

That's when the reality hit. This concept applies to every aspect of life. Some people start a small business, see it begin to take root, and then quit their full-time jobs before they know if their venture is truly going to be successful.

Others meet someone, fall in love, and rush into marriage before it's time. Still *otros* attempt a risky sport before they know all the rules of safety.

There is nothing wrong with wearing a life preserver. It was invented for a reason: to keep us safe and secure while we learn the rules of the water. A full-time job provides financial security while you chase your dream. Dating and getting to know each other provide a cushion of time and learning while a couple considers a more serious stage in their relationship. Safety measures in sports and other recreational pursuits keep us from harming ourselves. Don't take off the life jacket until it's absolutely the time to do so. If you do it prematurely, like my "nameless" sister, you risk plunging to the bottom of a lake, perhaps without a big *hermano o hermana* there to pull you up.

Dead fish and houseguests begin to stink after three days.

El muerto y el arrimado a los tres dias hieden.

As Austin Powers would say, "Ouch baby, very ouch." This *dicho* wastes no time in getting to the point. Know when to end your visit at someone's house.

Do not overstay your welcome and risk having this barbed Latino weapon aimed in your direction.

Too much constant contact raises a blister.

Mucho rozo levanta ampolla.

People who become "chummy" too quickly are likely to get on each other's nerves just as fast.

This could also be taken to mean that you must be on guard and avoid becoming a "pest," someone who is known as *encimozo,* an annoying hanger-on who is always around and doesn't give someone else any measure of privacy.

God smiles on he who thinks twice.

Del arrepentido se vale Dios.

This traditional *dicho* says you should not hesitate to "think twice" before making a major decision. You can even think three, four, or five times about it. It's your choice. You are in the driver's seat and no one needs to push you to make a final choice.

Si te arrepientes, if you decide not to move ahead, no problem. The proverb says God smiles on those who take the extra time and exercise caution in important matters.

With fear, you will do nothing.

Con el miedo no se hace nada.

If you inject a big measure of fear into everything you do then, in effect, you will do nothing. So many people walk around with *el miedo* playing a prominent role in their lives that it steals energy from them and robs them of the power to do their best.

Fear freezes. As I have told you before, sometimes it is good to have a little dose of fear or nervous energy run up and down your spine when you are facing a big event in your life. That excited emotional state is sometimes beneficial. It charges up your performance level and allows you to do the job with an extra boost of nervous energy.

But what if those nervous feelings and anxious moments get out of hand? *Esos nervios, los puedes controlar.* Those nerves, you can control. When I have a big meeting looming in the near future or a giant project that threatens to make my knees shake and my teeth chatter with nerves, I change my perspective. I don't aim for the meeting or the big project. I aim for the "day after." I place myself in that frame of time and ask myself the following question, "How relieved am I going to be when it's all over?" The answer is always, "very relieved" and that always serves to calm me down. I know deep inside that no matter how the meeting goes or how the project ends up that point of "tomorrow" will inevitably arrive. This serves to throw the fear off track because my mind is now focused on a time period that is not invested with the fear.

So don't walk around with *el miedo* blocking your path. Aim for tomorrow instead. That "tomorrow" is a land where you haven't allowed your fears to camp out.

No one is a purse of gold who is going to please everyone.

Nadie es monedita de oro para caerle bien a todo el mundo.

We spend our lives trying to make sure that we are liked by everyone. It's an exhausting and futile task. You can be as sweet and nice as Snow White, Mary Poppins, or even *Capurecita Roja* (Little Red Riding Hood) and someone is *still* going to think you are a jerk. That is just the way of the world.

Like this old *dicho* says, you can be exactly like a purse filled with gold and, even so, someone will have a problem with you. It's best to direct your energies somewhere else instead of constantly trying to be everyone's *favorita o favorito*.

If they'll do it for you, they'll do it to you.

Si lo hacen por tí, lo haran a tí.

"Oh baby, I love you. Of course I'll be with you forever. Come on, if nobody knows we're cheating, it's okay. I'm gonna leave them for you, baby. It's gonna be you and me." I may sound like a bitter guy with a pessimistic message but I have seen this happen too many times to count. Someone creates a tremendous emotional and personal upheaval in many lives by conducting affairs and romantic intrigue, apparently intoxicated on the drama. Then, when it's all over and things settle down, there is a little period of calm before it all gets repeated again. They never commit to anyone.

This handcrafted Chalupa Rule comes your way from the mouth of a friend who shared it with me. My wise, experienced friend looked at me and said, "Mario, if they do it *for* you, they'll do it *to* you."

Granted there are relationships that work in the wake of tumultuous breakups with previous partners. All this Rule advises is for you to exercise extreme caution in those situations.

Take the extra time and care in determining the person's true feelings. Do they love you? Or are they emotion junkies looking to get high off the drama created by a soap-opera love life?

Take on something harder than you already know how to do.

Intenta algo más difícil de lo que sabes hacer.

Do you always stay in the safe zone? Are three feet of water the deepest you will ever go into the pool? Then you are missing out. The only way to learn in life is to take on something much harder than you already know how to do. Weight lifters know that secret. They don't walk into a gym and repeatedly lift a ten-pound weight for the rest of their lives. They lift that light weight only for starters. Then, when they are ready, they move on to the heavier equipment. They always lift weights that are heavier than they are able to handle comfortably.

Their muscles sweat and strain but eventually the new weight becomes an old challenge, something conquered, a launching point for their new goal, something harder than they know how to lift.

Many of us go from day to day lifting the same weights at school or at work. Not even a drop of perspiration trails down our forehead. No sweat but a big problem. If a new challenge arises our mental muscles will be weak and unprepared for strain of the new, heavier weight we are asked to lift. Keep your muscles limber. It doesn't have to cost a penny. Do the crossword puzzle in the newspaper. Buy an inexpensive book and learn the basics of a new language. Teach yourself a few chords on the guitar. Stretch the muscles in *tu cabeza*. Take on something harder than you already know how to do.

From the front teeth outward.

De los dientes para afuera.

If you are accused of doing something, a favor for someone, a chore for a parent what ever it might be, *de los dientes para afuera*, it's a very bad thing. This means that you are not sincere in your actions. This *dicho* says if you are only going to perform a gesture from a hollow place of not caring, you might as well not perform it at all. You only show a surface emotion. You are shallow and lack depth of feeling. At its most basic meaning, this saying indicates that you are only putting in enough effort from the "front teeth outward."

Put your ideas on "layaway."

Pon tus ideas en "layaway."

Okay, so you have this great idea that is going to change the world and reinvent the wheel. The problem is, you don't have the money or other resources to pull it off. Wait! *Espera.* Don't throw that idea in the trash just yet.

As children, the concept of "layaway" was the only financial avenue to make large purchases. My parents would set aside school clothes or other items and pay them off, a small payment at a time. Before we knew it, we had our clothes for school.

The same goes for your "big ideas." Think back to all the times some innovative product or "new way of doing things" popped into your *cabeza.* I can almost hear you saying, "Nah. It will never work." And then, that is it. As we used to say at the end of story time, *Colorin, Colorado, este cuento se ha acabado.* It's the Latino equivalent of "They all lived happily ever after." But you don't live happily ever after. Some subconscious little bug is always there wondering "What if?"

Get a little notepad and a pen. Carry it around with you at all times. When something comes to mind, write it down. Even if it is the silliest idea in the world, put it down on *un papel.* Some of the world's biggest inventions have come out of crazy ideas. Who would have thought of Liquid Paper or Silly String? People have made *mucho dinero* with those ideas. When you fill up that notebook, put it away somewhere.

That way, your ideas are on "layaway" until some time in the future when you open the book and realize that the time has come to put some of those thoughts into action.

You took time and brain power to create the idea. Give it enough *respeto* to put it on paper. You validate your thought processes and encourage your *mente* to come up with more brainstorms, perhaps a whole new way to make *tortillas*. Put your ideas on "layaway"!

If you can't control something, go to the movies.

Si no tienes control sobre algo, al cine.

The Chalupa Rules learned this wonderful, stress-busting technique from a cultured, worldly Manhattan gentleman.

The Chalupa Rules was invited to a fancy party way up in the New York skyline, at a penthouse that would leave you with your *lengua*, your tongue, hanging out of your mouth. The apartment was filled with antiques, priceless paintings, and a grand piano. A grand piano. How did they get that enormous musical instrument up to that soaring, breathtaking residence? I couldn't help it. I asked the question. The gentleman looked at me, smiled, took a deep, elegant breath and said, "I went to the movies." I didn't understand what he was saying either. Went to the movies? What kind of an answer is that? Noticing that my eyebrows were now suspended somewhere over my head in confusion, he continued.

The story went as follows. He had wanted a grand piano his entire life. He decided that when he could afford it that was exactly the purchase he was going to make.

Little did he realize that when he was finally able to make his dream come true, he lived way up in the sky in a penthouse that sometimes got lost in the clouds. Still, this gentleman would not let go of his *sueño*. He was going to have his grand piano.

He selected the piano, paid for it, and went home to wait for his prize to be delivered. That's when he says all hell broke loose. Furious, frantic phone calls flew between building management and the piano store. How were they going to get that piano up into *el cielo*?

That's when my new *amigo*, even though he is this fancy, New York Manhattan *gringo*, dreamed up his very own Chalupa Rule.

He said that since he had absolutely no control over how the piano was going to make it up to his apartment, he wasn't going to worry about it. He says, "Mario, I simply went to the movies and when I got back to my apartment, the piano was there."

I love that story. There is definitely a Chalupa Rule power in his words. There are situations in life when, no matter how hard we try to affect the outcome, nothing will change. We cannot always change someone's mind. We are not always able to solve a problem that others are already trying to solve anyway.

We can't waste energy, time, and emotion on moving a "Rock of Gibraltar" that is out of our league. What this gentleman's Chalupa Rule tells us is to chill out and let the experts do their work. Trust in others' talents and skills. Step out of the way and let them do the jobs they are trained to perform.

Instead of running around, wringing his hands and worrying about how the piano would be transported, this guy had the right idea.

He went to the movies.

So, when something is overwhelming and I have no control over the outcome, I go to the movies as well. You don't have to physically go to the movies, although it is a nice idea. This is just a phrase that says pull your energy out of the battle, hang up your weapons and your Albert Einstein thinking cap, and let others' Chalupa Rules save the day.

The job interview is over and you have to wait for a final decision? Go to the movies. You've turned in your final semester project and are waiting for the grade? Go to the movies. You've bought a large piece of furniture and have hired experts to get it up the stairs? Go to the movies.

Big problem? Can't do anything about it? Don't sweat it. Go to the movies.

Thank you Mister-Fancy-New-York-*Gringo* for a refreshing, stress-relieving Chalupa Rule that proves you do not have to be a Latino in order to invent a homemade, handcrafted guide to life.

Hasta pronto amigos.

You can contact me at www.chaluparules.com.

CHAPTER THIRTY-ONE

Your "Handcrafted" Chalupa Rules

1. **Draw** an *imagen*, an image that best symbolizes your Chalupa Rule.

2. **Write** the name of the image below your drawing.

3. **Next**, write the Chalupa Rule in Spanish and English in the lines provided.

4. **Use** the lines provided to fill in the meaning of your homemade Chalupa rule.

5. **Live** the Chalupa Rule every day!

The Meaning of My Chalupa Rule:

_____
_____
_____
_____
_____
_____
_____
_____
_____
_____
_____

The Meaning of My Chalupa Rule:

_____

_____

_____

_____

_____

_____

_____

_____

_____

_____

_____

_____

_____

_____

The Meaning of My Chalupa Rule:

_____

_____

_____

_____

The Meaning of My Chalupa Rule:

_____

_____

_____

_____

_____

_____

_____

_____

_____

_____

_____

_____

_____

_____

The Meaning of My Chalupa Rule:

_____

_____

_____

_____

_____

_____

_____

_____

_____

_____

_____

The Meaning of My Chalupa Rule:

_____

_____

_____

_____

_____

_____

_____

_____

_____

_____

_____

_____

The Meaning of My Chalupa Rule:

_____

_____

_____

_____

_____

_____

_____

_____

_____

_____

_____

_____

_____

A portion of the proceeds from *The Chalupa Rules* will go to:
The Hispanic Association of Colleges and Universities
www.hacu.org

The Humane Society of New York
www.humanesocietyny.org

Do have questions about life in *Gringolandia*?
Send your questions to **askmario@chaluparules.com**

For appearance and speaking engagement information go to:
www.chaluparules.com

ABOUT THE AUTHOR

Mario Bósquez is coanchor of *CBS 2 News This Morning* on WCBS in New York City. With over twenty-five years in television, Mario has covered the World Trade Center disaster and Pope John Paul II's trip to Cuba. His reports from the 1999 Columbia earthquake earned him an award from Americares and President George Bush, Sr. He has also been recognized by the City of New York for his work as a Latino journalist.

A novelist and award-winning playwright, Mario's play *Los Duendes/The Restless Spirits* has been performed in Houston and New York City. The South Texas native speaks to students about the importance of education. A stand-up comic, Mario also performs in clubs and festivals in New York and Chicago.

Mario resides in New York City, where he supports the Humane Society and perfects the art of take-out food with emphasis on Chinese and Tex-Mex lunch specials.